LIFE'S 101 GREATEST SECRETS

Dr Srinath Sridharan has been a trusted strategic counsel to leading corporates for nearly three decades, with expertise spanning transformation initiatives, succession planning and business scaling. He serves as an independent director across multiple industries, and also as executive coach to senior leaders, guiding them towards impactful leadership. A prolific columnist and sought-after thought leader, he frequently addresses corporate boards and family councils on critical issues.

Srinath is the author of *Family and Dhanda*, a highly acclaimed book on family businesses. He is also the co-editor and co-author of *Time for Bharat*, as well as the co-author of *Newsprint to Heartprint* and *Reimagining ESG*. He is a visiting fellow at the Observer Research Foundation and a guest faculty member at prominent academic and regulatory institutions.

Reach him at:
X: @ssmumbai
Insta: @AuthorSrinath
LinkedIn: https://in.linkedin.com/in/srinathsridharan

LIFE'S 101 GREATEST SECRETS FOR A RICHER, HAPPIER YOU

SRINATH SRIDHARAN

RUPA

Published by
Rupa Publications India Pvt. Ltd 2025
161-B/4, Gulmohar House,
Yusuf Sarai Community Centre,
New Delhi 110049

Sales centres:
Bengaluru Chennai
Hyderabad Kolkata Mumbai

The views and opinions expressed in this book are the author's own and the facts are as reported by him; these have been verified to the extent possible, and the publishers are not in any way liable for the same.

P-ISBN: 978-93-7003-963-6
E-ISBN: 978-93-7003-592-8

First impression 2025

10 9 8 7 6 5 4 3 2 1

Printed in India

For

Ninupta and Sannuta

You make me stay true to everything.
You are my moral compass.
After all, 'the child is father of the man.'
Remember, you are not just what you are now.
What you were, or did, achieved or did not, do not count.
If you can shape what you want to be, with what you are now,
that would be the way to what you want to be.
This book is for you.

Contents

Preface

Life is a curious thing, isn't it?

We are handed a bewildering array of experiences, moments and lessons, most of which arrive without warning, as if we were simply meant to figure them out on our own. Yet, somewhere along the way, we discover that it's not the great achievements or the loud accolades that define us, but the quiet, often overlooked lessons—those small, seemingly insignificant moments that are somehow more profound than anything else—that shape our journey.

When I was asked how I would like to celebrate my fiftieth birthday, my response was: 'I don't want any celebration.' It wasn't because I didn't appreciate life, but because I had reached a point where gratitude was my overwhelming feeling. Gratitude for my existence. Gratitude for having come back from the brink of hardship and struggle. But as life has taught me, never say never, and never assume that the worst is over. Nor should you ever believe that the best will come automatically.

The truth is, life is about focusing on positivity and making an effort to keep moving forward, no matter how painful or hard it may seem. The effort, in the end, is worth every moment.

More than eighty per cent of humanity lives beyond

the age of fifty, yet I know I am among the lucky ones. Every year, over 160 million people do not make it to this age due to reasons beyond their control—wars, strife, diseases, and more. That alone fills me with gratitude for being alive, for being here, and for being able to write these words.

What do I want to leave behind for my children, beyond what every parent would naturally wish to leave behind? This book is an attempt to tell my children—and all children—that they matter, that their thoughts, their deeds, and their actions matter in this world.

In a world with billions of people, it's easy to feel insignificant. But each of us has a role, a purpose, and a chance to make a difference. This book is for them—a testament to the fact that they matter, and they are valuable.

We are all born with our own version of an 'ovarian lottery'. The family we are born into shapes much of our journey—whether we like it or not. It's not something we can control. We don't choose our parents, our birthplace, or the circumstances that shape us. Some might call it karma, while others might term it destiny. Be that as it may, it plays a powerful role in shaping who we become.

Life is a series of ups and downs. It's full of challenges, but also of moments of joy. How we navigate these trials and find the strength to move through and beyond them is the true test of a human being. Spirituality, I believe, gives us a compass, helping us steer our way forward without losing sight of material comforts or human connections. But that balance is delicate.

I wish I could call my journey thus far a 'fine innings', much like a cricket commentator would. There have been slow moments, bumps along the way, and sparks of brilliance. There have been near-death experiences and unexpected turns, all in the life of someone who never had a fair shot at the success he somehow achieved. Think of my journey as that of an average cricketer, but one who's been blessed with a little luck, some great mentors, and plenty of lessons learnt along the way.

As I reflect on my own journey, I find that the best lessons didn't come from textbooks or from well-meaning advice forced upon me, but the ones I learnt the hard way—the ones I had to learn with skin in the game, sometimes painfully so. It's funny, isn't it? We spend much of our youth chasing after answers to questions we can't fully understand even now. Then, as we grow older, we realize that the answers were never in those questions in the first place. They were in the messy, imperfect, and often unpredictable path that led us to where we are now.

Life's 101 Greatest Secrets for a Richer, Happier You, a collection of lessons gleaned from the lives of towering personalities across various walks of life, is not meant to be a guidebook to a perfect life—that's an impossible dream. What it offers, however, are simple truths, insights and realizations that, once truly understood, can help steer us in the right direction, one step at a time. They can give us the happiness, will and strength to accept life as it is.

Yes, there will be times when you read these lessons and think, 'Oh, that sounds easier than it actually is!' And you will be right, of course. Life's challenges are never straightforward, but the power lies in how we rise above them and carry on, sometimes even laughing at ourselves in the process.

In this book, I draw on examples of individuals, including celebrities, whose stories illustrate valuable life lessons through their positivity and resilience. These lessons celebrate their achievements against all odds and serve as inspiring reflections of the qualities that helped them, not as endorsements of them.

So, as you journey through these pages, try and take what resonates with you, and perhaps—just perhaps—find comfort in knowing that the road is long, but you are certainly not walking it alone. After all, these are lessons we all must learn, even if it means taking a few detours along the way.

This book is for a happier you.

1

Nothing shines better on you than your self-confidence.

The world is not there to help you get it.
It's called *self*-confidence for a reason.
You need to find it within your*self.*

Life is not a popularity poll. So, don't chase adulation from others.

The mind is the most powerful tool we possess; it shapes our perceptions, influences our decisions, and ultimately determines our actions—or inactions. Our thoughts create our reality, setting the stage for how we respond to challenges, opportunities, and even setbacks. If we believe in our abilities, we're more likely to take confident steps toward our goals. Conversely, self-doubt or negative thinking can hold us back, leading to hesitation or even inaction.

When we learn to cultivate a positive mindset, and see obstacles as opportunities and failures as lessons, we empower ourselves to act with purpose. By cultivating resilience, optimism and self-belief, we can break through mental blocks and unlock our full potential. In the end, it's all in our mind—the thoughts we nurture, the beliefs we hold, and the attitudes we choose, that drive the life we lead.

Muhammad Ali is the perfect example of someone who embodied the life lesson that nothing shines better than self-confidence. Known for his bold declarations, like 'I am the greatest,' Ali never waited for the world to validate him. He had an unshakeable belief in himself, long before he became a three-time world heavyweight champion. Early in his career, people often mocked his self-assurance, terming it as arrogance, but Ali understood that his self-confidence was his strength. He once said, 'It's the repetition of affirmations that leads to belief. And once that belief becomes a deep conviction, things begin to happen.' Ali knew that, regardless of public opinion or approval, his success depended on his personal conviction. His journey reminds us that confidence truly comes from within, and when you believe in yourself, you light up in a way that no external validation can provide.

2

Nothing adds lustre to life better than truth and humility.

Plain unadulterated truth. And humility.

F the world for a minute.

Well, that 'F' was 'forget'.

For most people, truth is bitter and ugly. In general, they prefer optical and auditory illusions. When someone asks you, 'How are you doing?', have you tried saying, 'Oh terrible. I am not well and I need…'?

That might be one of the last times you would be invited anywhere again.

But in the long run, truth is simpler.

Easier, on your emotions.

Lighter, on your conscience.

Wear it well. On your sleeve.

One of the most inspiring examples of humility and truthfulness is Mahatma Gandhi, the leader of India's non-violent struggle for independence from British rule. He changed the course of history not through force, but through his unwavering commitment to truth, peace, and civil disobedience—always rooting himself in simplicity and honesty, choosing handspun cloth over riches, silence over noise, and service over power, reminding the world that true greatness lies in living by one's values, not in titles or positions. He often referred to himself as a 'seeker of truth' and believed in 'Satyagraha', which translates to 'holding firmly to truth'. Despite his fame and influence, Gandhi lived modestly, dressed in simple khadi clothing, and took responsibility for his errors, constantly reflecting on his actions. He believed that to truly inspire and lead, one had to be truthful to oneself and humble in one's dealings with others. His humility allowed people to connect with him on a deeply human level, and his honesty shone brighter than any title or position he could have held. Gandhi's life reminds us that truth and humility are what elevate a person's spirit, adding lasting brilliance to their legacy.

Being humble is a way to show your respect to others, across the hierarchies that society creates.

I have seen many successful individuals using a simple method to approach others. So, a mantra I have used and shared many times is: 'Treat others the way you want to be treated.'

To begin with, I grew up in a home filled with love—a kind of intergenerational warmth and affection that held us all together. But somewhere along the way, things changed. Family disputes cropped up, lines were drawn, and the bonds that once felt so strong started to weaken. With that shift, I understood what it meant to lack the privileges some family members enjoyed: the security that financial resources provide, the comfort of social standing, and the invaluable support that even one well-connected uncle or aunt might offer. I remember wondering, with a touch of bitterness, why no one stepped in to help cover part of my education expenses—a sum that was small change to them. But life doesn't always provide ready answers; instead, it shapes you.

So I learnt perseverance. I learnt to rely on myself, even if it meant others found me distant or reserved. In the end, it was someone outside the core family who enabled my education, a quiet act of generosity that left a lasting mark. So, when I say 'success is relative', the slight cheekiness and pun are intended. I mean, who needs family ties to define or ensure success, anyway?

3

Success and money do matter.

It is okay to be rich, to be more than *average rich.* Or *want* to be rich. It is not okay not to have stable finances. Forget the rest of the world, even you can't survive in this material world without resources.

I learnt it the hard way. Fortunately, coming from the background that I did, I didn't do anything stupid, immoral or illegal.

Oprah Winfrey's journey shows the importance of success and financial stability, especially when you've known struggle. Raised in poverty and facing countless obstacles, Oprah understood from a young age that if she wanted to escape her circumstances, she had to build a successful career and create her own wealth. She did just that, rising to become one of the most influential media personalities worldwide, and one of the first African-American women billionaires. But Oprah never forgot her roots; she often speaks about how her financial success enables her to give back, to provide opportunities for others who face similar hardships. Her story is a testament to the fact that while money itself isn't the key to happiness, having it can offer security, freedom, and a platform to create positive change. Success and money matter, not just for ourselves, but for what we can do with them for others.

In today's world, having financial resources is important. Financial security matters. So, don't be under the illusion that knowledge or education alone will sustain you. What truly counts is how you apply what you have learnt, and how you turn your skills, wisdom and insights into value for others, and in doing so, create value for yourself.

Wanting to be successful in the material world can be an important motivator. But let it not push you into doing or thinking wrong, or towards destroying your core values.

But remember, success is not a guaranteed sign of happiness, peace of mind, or lasting growth. True fulfilment comes from alignment between what you do, how you live, and who you are becoming—beyond just what you achieve.

Fight hard and fair for your success, *and financial dues.* People and societies are fair not by design, and at every turn, there may be someone out to short-change you. So, claim your dues, when it is time.

Another key lesson is to understand that success is rarely, if ever, achieved overnight. The entrepreneur, artist, or athlete hailed as an 'instant success' likely spent years working tirelessly, overcoming setbacks, and honing their skills to reach their goals. Every failure along the way was a step towards building their inner strength and drive. As Vince Lombardi wisely said, 'It's not whether you get knocked down. It's whether you get up.' Finally, cultivating passion, compassion, and purpose brings meaning to our lives. Passion fuels us beyond the physical, pushing us toward our goals with energy and focus. It's through passion that we find a sense of purpose, fulfilment, and the motivation to impact the world in a positive way.

4

Formal education alone won't help you in life.

It may probably for your first job and for an alumni network.

Skills will help you.

Networks will.

Street smartness will.

Travel will. Travel like crazy. With what you can afford. Be open to what is in the world, and around you.

Richard Branson is a fine example of how formal education alone isn't the key to success. Leaving school at sixteen, he started his first business—a magazine called Student—with no formal business education. But Branson had curiosity, grit, and the drive to make things happen. He learnt quickly from experience, surrounding himself with people who had skills he didn't, and constantly pushed himself out of his comfort zone. From selling records to founding Virgin Atlantic, he thrived on travelling, exploring new ideas, and developing an instinct for spotting opportunity. Branson's journey illustrates that while education can open doors, real growth often comes from life's experience, developing skills on the go, and connecting with people who broaden our horizons. Travel, relationships, and a willingness to try again, despite failing, have been Branson's biggest teachers—and he's proof that while school can be valuable, life itself is the greatest classroom.

Constant skilling will be a necessity.

Digital literacy will be crucial for you.

Financial literacy will give you financial independence.

Constantly upgrade your knowledge, skills, network.

Be relevant wherever you are—at work, at home or in a friends' network.

Be thorough in what you know. Keep improving on what you know.

And this has to be done with your own truth and values intact.

5

Resist cheating. Of any kind.

It's easy to cheat.

In a card game.

In the boardroom.

In business.

In life.

In relationships.

But it will hurt you. And hit you hard someday.

As hard as the hardest time you have ever had.

So, simply don't cheat.

A famous example of integrity in the face of temptation is Warren Buffett. Known for his ethical approach to business, Buffett has always emphasized honesty as a cornerstone of his success. Early in his career, he was offered many shortcuts and questionable opportunities, but he consistently chose the harder, ethical path. Buffett often says that integrity is like a financial 'reputation account'—it takes years to build, but one wrong move can drain it in an instant. Whether in boardrooms or investments, he has resisted the urge to cut corners or cheat. His unwavering commitment to honesty has earned him not only massive success but also the trust and admiration of millions. Buffett's journey is a reminder that while cheating might seem easy for the moment, it undermines long-term success and damages the very foundation of who we are.

6

It's okay to make mistakes.

Forgive yourself.
Don't forget the lesson learnt from that mistake, and turn it into your strength.
Correct your mistake at once. Correcting a mistake starts with accepting it.
Be it a work judgement.
Be it an emotional rapport.
Be it your workplace.
Be it in your relationships.

A powerful example of learning from mistakes and moving forward comes from Steve Jobs, co-founder of Apple. Early in his career, Jobs was known for his intense passion but also his sometimes, difficult personality, which eventually led to his ouster from Apple in 1985—a painful public setback for him. Rather than letting this failure define him, Jobs reflected on his mistakes and used this period to grow. He went on to create NeXT and buy Pixar, both ventures that expanded his skills and vision. By the time he returned to Apple in 1997, he had not only learnt to refine his leadership approach but also built the resilience that would drive Apple's iconic resurgence. Jobs often spoke about how that painful chapter taught him invaluable lessons about humility, persistence, and innovation. It's a reminder that mistakes don't end the journey; they redirect it if we're willing to pause, learn, and come back stronger.

7

Be grateful.

I have to thank each one of those individuals whom I know, knew, am in touch with, am not in touch with, who were acquaintances, whom I can't relate to anymore or who can't relate to me anymore—all those relationships where distance or time has crept in.

I am what and who I am, simply as a combination of every single transaction and experience in life.

Some very positive.

Some exponential in their contribution.

Some negative.

I am grateful for every moment.

Good, bad, terrible, fantastic. They are words to express emotions about those moments.

But I am grateful.

For I live every moment with gratitude.

Especially after certain incidents in my forties, for I think I finally am maturing into a human being.

No wonder, I have always had an inner voice telling me for decades that I am a bit slow on the uptake!

I remember a time in my forties when life seemed to test me in every way possible. It was a period of setbacks—some personal, some professional—that left me feeling as though the ground beneath me had vanished. I was wrestling with loss, confusion, and a sense of disillusionment that clouded everything I knew. One evening, feeling particularly low, I decided to pause and simply acknowledge what was still there: family, a few close friends, my health, even the lessons these challenges were forcing me to learn. I began ending each day with a quiet 'thank you' to the universe, no matter how hard it was to find the silver lining. Slowly, that small ritual changed me. The more I focused on what I had, rather than on what I'd lost, the lighter I felt. It was in those humbling moments that I realized true gratitude—an anchor in the storm, one that grounds you and keeps you moving forward.

Look, I didn't wake up one day at fifty magically full of wisdom. It sneaks up on you—somewhere between paying EMIs, making many mistakes, and pretending to understand new slang. If you're in your teens, twenty or thirty now, you're still in the thick of building, breaking, figuring things out. I was too. But here's the wild part: one day, you realize you've actually learnt a few things. Not because you read them in a book, but because life smacked you with them a few dozen times. The best part? You finally start caring less about impressing people and more about sleeping well, eating on time, and staying away from unnecessary drama. Trust me, that's progress. Hang in there. You'll get here too. And when you do, you'll laugh at how seriously you took everything in your twenties. That's the secret gift of age and experiences: clarity.

Say a prayer of gratitude every night, whether you are religious or follow a specific *-ism.* Nothing else matters. Think of it as sending positive energy to the universe.

8

Be kind.

It does not cost anything.

But it may test your patience.

People will pass judgement on your every act of kindness.

They will suspect the intention; they will wonder if you have an ulterior motive.

Sometimes, kindness is mistaken for selfishness, because people struggle to believe that generosity can be without agenda. In a world where so many interactions are transactional, people often search for the 'price tag' behind an act of kindness, forgetting that true kindness asks for nothing in return. Let them think what they will—your intention is what matters.

Just be kind.

It makes you a student of life who is forever curious, and you learn to be human.

Kindness is often thought of in terms of grand gestures, but the smallest, most personal act can leave the deepest impact. It can be as simple as offering a word of encouragement to someone who is struggling, reminding them of their worth when they feel down and out. Kindness might mean listening attentively when someone needs to unburden, or just sitting in silence beside them, offering quiet companionship in a moment of sadness. Kindness is the gentle reassurance of a friend's touch, or even a smile shared with a stranger, that brightens up their day. True kindness doesn't always require material resources; just your presence, empathy, and willingness to show up for others in ways that speak to their heart, suffice. Whether with words, time, or a comforting gesture, kindness is an act of connection that can heal and uplift in countless ways.

Indian business leader Azim Premji, known for his quiet yet profound acts of kindness, exemplifies how to stay kind even when your intentions are questioned. As one of India's most generous philanthropists, Premji has donated a substantial part of his wealth through the Azim Premji Foundation, focusing on education and healthcare. Some have wondered why a business tycoon would part with so much of his fortune, even wondering if there is a hidden agenda. Yet, Premji remains steadfast, choosing kindness as a means of giving back to the country that enabled his success.

9

Never betray anyone's trust.

Trust is one of the most valuable bonds you can share with another person. Once given, it's a sign of faith, respect, and vulnerability. Betraying someone's trust is easy, but rebuilding it is often impossible. When you betray someone's trust, you damage the foundation of your relationship and inflict wounds that time alone may not heal.

A life lesson I've come to hold close to my heart is to honour the trust others place in me. It means being reliable, honest, and considerate in my actions and words.

Keeping trust intact strengthens relationships, builds character, and cultivates a life of integrity.

Never betray anyone's trust—it's a commitment that reflects who you are and the values you stand by. Trust isn't built only in grand gestures; it's reinforced in the small, consistent ways you show up for people, keep your word, and respect confidences.

Oprah Winfrey, a global icon, built her media empire based on the trust she has earned from her audience. She has always been transparent about her struggles, vulnerabilities and mistakes, ensuring her viewers feel a genuine connection. Oprah once said that breaking someone's trust would mean losing the essence of her bond with her followers—a price she would never be willing to pay.

10

I am allowed to change my opinion if data point changes.

You can have an opinion based on what you know, and how you analyse it. But it is absolutely fine to change your opinion, as your learning and data points change.

A great example of the power of adapting to new information is Mahatma Gandhi. Though he began his early professional life as a barrister who largely supported the British legal system, Gandhi's views shifted dramatically as he witnessed the oppression and injustice faced by Indians in South Africa, and later in India. Initially, he believed in working within British structures for reform, but as he experienced the reality of colonial rule, his stance evolved. He championed non-violent resistance and civil disobedience, approaches he refined and transformed over time as he observed what was most effective for India's freedom struggle. Gandhi's journey shows that it's not only acceptable but wise to adapt our beliefs when faced with new experiences or data. It's our strength, not our weakness, to evolve thoughtfully—it means we're listening, learning, and ready to grow.

11

I can form my own rapport, relationship and equation that are different from what others have in my family.

You don't need to have the same friends or enemies that your family has. You can differ from your family in your rapport with people; your rapport is based on your own journey.

You are in charge of your own life. You are not bound by any familial, societal strings to tie you down to a decision on forging human relationships. You have to make your own choices about who you relate to, and how intensely you build your rapport with whom.

However, be ready to face others' emotions—from anger to scorn to neglect. But then, don't take either emotion too seriously.

Sometimes, the wisdom you need doesn't come from just one person. It comes from watching how different people handle the same situation—and realizing you can borrow a bit from each, or choose a path that none of them took. You are allowed more than one role model. And you are allowed to make up your own mind.

That includes the way you relate to others. You don't have to inherit your family's friendships, rivalries, judgements, or emotional debts. Your rapport with someone can—and often should—be different from the one your parents or siblings had. You're not disloyal for seeing someone differently, nor are you obliged to carry another person's version of history.

You are, at every point, free to build your own relationships. Your sense of ease or unease, your shared memories, your mutual respect—those are yours to navigate. These bonds are formed through your journey, not your family's. And that journey may look nothing like theirs.

Yes, this will sometimes come at a cost. People may not understand. They may question your loyalty, accuse you of naivety, or simply distance themselves. That's okay. Not everyone will see what you see, or feel what you feel. Don't let their confusion become your guilt.

Take people as they come. Let your relationships breathe on their own terms. You will find that over time, those you've chosen to see with fresh eyes—and those who've chosen to do the same with you—become your chosen family in quiet, profound ways.

12

Family is important. It's about sanity.

What truly defines family—be it siblings and parents, spouse, children, in-laws, and those extended cousins and cousins-in-law—will be determined with time. So will your acceptance of them and vice versa.

But you need to define what constitutes your core.

Those few members who matter.

Whose words and actions or lack thereof will matter to you.

The rest are co-passengers in a journey.

After the journey, you rarely keep in touch with them.

An inspiring example of this life lesson is Amitabh Bachchan, the iconic Bollywood actor. Known for his close-knit family, he has always placed immense value on his relationship with his parents, wife Jaya, children Abhishek and Shweta, and their families. Through life's ups and downs—career highs, financial troubles, health challenges, family milestones, among others—Bachchan has shown that family is his anchor. He shared a very strong bond with his father, the poet and writer Harivansh Rai Bachchan, who deeply influenced him; even years after his father's passing, he often quotes his words of wisdom, and cherishes their shared values.

Though Bachchan is connected to many in the industry and society, it's evident that his core circle remains small, and it's their support that matters most to him. In a world of fame and constant public scrutiny, he has maintained this inner sanctuary, proving that while many may come and many may go, true family—the ones you hold closest to your heart—is irreplaceable.

13

Don't fear failure. It is the best teacher.

Wisdom isn't found in quick quotes, catchy phrases, or neatly packaged advice. It doesn't come from the pages of most 'self-help' books, which often simplify the depth of real learning. True wisdom comes from an active life—a life where you explore, take risks, and learn from the setbacks and challenges along the way. Those who live passively, letting life happen to them, miss out on these valuable lessons.

Don't fear failure; it is one of the best teachers. Instead, you must fear *never failing* because that would mean you *never tried*. Embrace every opportunity to learn, grow, and become wiser through experience.

Dr A.P.J. Abdul Kalam, former President of India, had his fair share of failures early in his career, especially during some critical stages of India's space and missile programmes. One notable instance was in 1979, when the SLV-3 rocket, India's first satellite, failed to reach the orbit, leading to a highly publicized setback. Dr Kalam, who helmed the project, was deeply disappointed but took full responsibility. Instead of fearing the fallout, he learnt from every aspect of that failure, working tirelessly with his team to rectify the issues. The following year, the team successfully launched the SLV-3, marking India's entry into the space age. Kalam often spoke about how that failure shaped his outlook—it instilled in him fortitude, groundedness, and an enduring commitment to keep striving. His journey became a testament to how failure can pave the way for future achievements when approached with the right mindset—the willingness to learn.

14

Focus on more than just a career.

Being independent financially is important. But money can't buy you peace of mind or sleep. Perhaps, it can buy you ways and means to both, or material comfort.

Have your own social identity. A stable career can help reinforce such an identity.

But then have your personal identity too, of who you are, without seeking refuge only behind a professional identity.

That is the challenge. And the danger. That we get delusional about who we are *professionally*.

Indra Nooyi, former CEO of PepsiCo, embodies the importance of staying focused on career and financial independence while maintaining one's unique identity. Growing up in a middle-class family in India, she pursued her education fiercely, eventually becoming one of the most powerful women in the corporate world. Her career not only provided financial stability but also empowered her to challenge stereotypes and redefine leadership on her own terms. Even at the height of her success, Nooyi remained grounded in her values and identity, famously carrying her cultural heritage with pride. She balanced her demanding career with personal responsibilities, proving that a strong professional identity can coexist with a rich, personal sense of self. Through her journey, she shows that financial independence and a fulfilling career are essential, but they are strongest when balanced with an unwavering commitment to who you are at your core.

15

Build a network. Especially when you don't begin with inherited advantage.

In both life and career, access matters. Often, it's not just what you know, but who is willing to vouch for you, respond to you, or open a door when you knock. For those who haven't inherited influential connections or elite affiliations, building a network is a necessity. Not as a transactional pursuit, but as a human one.

One of the most underappreciated yet transformative skills in this process is the ability to truly listen. To be interested, rather than to always aim to be interesting, is a quiet superpower. It signals maturity, builds trust, and opens space for deeper connection. Listening—not the performative kind, but the patient, curious, fully present kind—helps people feel seen. And when people feel seen, they remember you.

In both personal and professional spaces, it's this kind of sincere engagement that becomes the foundation of meaningful relationships. It's not about collecting contacts. It's about earning confidence. When you listen well, you often understand more than what's being said, and that kind of awareness is invaluable.

And make no mistake: building a network requires energy. Consistent, generous, human energy. Not the noisy kind, but the kind that remembers a name, checks in without agenda, offers help without waiting for leverage. That effort compounds over time, quietly but powerfully.

N.R. Narayana Murthy, co-founder of Infosys, is a fine example of this principle in action. Coming from modest beginnings, without the conventional markers of pedigree or inherited capital, he understood that credibility is often built through relationships. From clients to colleagues, he invested in people by listening, learning, and engaging with sincerity. He didn't enter rooms with influence; he built influence by the way he showed up in those rooms. His network was the outcome of intent, respect, and presence.

A network is not just a ladder to climb. It is a root system that grounds and sustains you through different seasons of life. The people who matter to you at twenty may not be the ones who shape you at forty, and that's not disloyalty, it's growth. Don't mistake visibility for connection; real relationships aren't built through performance but through presence and quiet consistency. In a world that often overvalues visibility, it's important to remember that being heard starts with being genuinely interested in hearing others. That is how networks are built and sustained.

16

Acquaintances, always. Anchors, rarely.

You.
Your closest family.
A few friends.
The rest are passersby in your life. Just as you are, in their lives.

Over the course of a lifetime, you will meet thousands of people. Some will walk with you for a few steps, some for a few years, but only a rare handful will walk with you through fire and fog. You'll have countless acquaintances, many friends, and endless well-wishers in good times. But your true circle—the one that holds when everything else falls away—will likely fit on one hand. You. Your innermost family. A few friends, if you're lucky. The rest, however warm or well-meaning, are passersby. Just as you are, in their lives. It's not cynical. It's just how human lives flow: converging, intersecting, drifting.

Former first lady of the United States Michelle Obama has often spoken about this with remarkable clarity. Through decades in public life, she has been surrounded by attention, applause and access. Yet, she frequently returns to the idea that her emotional safety net has always been small. Her mother, her brother, a few college friends, her daughters, and Barack—that's her real circle. The people who knew her before the spotlight and never saw her differently after it. During moments of personal doubt, political storms and intense public scrutiny, it was this circle—not the world—that helped her stay grounded, honest and whole.

The lesson isn't about distrusting people. It's about knowing where to rest your soul. You don't have to shut the world out. But you do need to know where your centre is. Value the wide circle, engage with joy and openness. Just don't mistake proximity for permanence. The core will always be few. That's not a flaw of human connection. That's its narrative.

17

Don't merely look at presence or participation. Impact matters.

You're not here just to show up like an Olympian claiming that participation is the prize.

The truth is, no one remembers who came second, let alone eleventh.

But what people do remember is how you made them feel—through a kind gesture, your quiet honesty, or your unadorned simplicity. That's what earns respect, friendships, and a lasting impression.

Virat Kohli, a global cricket icon, is a prime example of someone prioritizing impact over mere participation. Known for his relentless pursuit of excellence, Kohli doesn't settle for just showing up or participating; he aims to make every innings count. His commitment to fitness, discipline, and mental toughness has set new standards in Indian cricket, inspiring teammates and fans alike. Kohli's focus has always been on delivering impactful performances—winning games for his team, breaking records, and setting an example of consistency. While there are many players on the field, Kohli's emphasis on impact has made him a standout, remembered not just for his presence but for changing the game in lasting ways.

18

Nothing is permanent.

Be it the friendship you swore by as being lifelong, that probably did not stand the test of distance, or even marriage for that matter—nothing lasts forever.

Importantly, friendship is not about hierarchy. The only friendship that matters is a relationship of equals. Not equal in wealth or in competence. But in the foundation of such a friendship.

Shah Rukh Khan, often hailed as the 'King of Bollywood', has experienced the transitory nature of friendship, fame, and success in a deeply personal way. Starting out as an outsider in the industry, he formed close bonds with colleagues, some of whom became like family. Over time, as life and careers changed, some of those bonds evolved or faded. Despite the shifting circles around him, Khan has stayed grounded by focusing on the relationships that truly matter to him—his family and a few trusted friends who share a foundation of mutual respect, not based on status or success but on shared values. Through it all, he has often spoken about how life's impermanence has taught him inner strength and humility, a reminder that fame and friendships can be fleeting but the bonds rooted in authenticity remain.

19

When life surprises you.

Just when you think you've figured life out, it rewrites the script. Not all surprises come with fireworks—some arrive quietly, as people you never thought would matter suddenly do. And some who once held centre stage quietly slip into the wings. That is the strange beauty of life. It doesn't follow a fixed storyline, and you're not the only one taken by surprise.

There was a time when I believed some relationships would never falter. That a few people were forever. They weren't. Yet when they drifted, others stepped in—sometimes those I barely knew, who showed up with unexpected warmth, perspective or even help. Strangers became anchors. Chance meetings became lifelines. Disappointments were replaced not with bitterness, but with new beginnings.

Life has its seasons. And each season carries its own cast of characters. Some stay for spring, others walk with you through the storms of monsoon. You won't always know why people come or go—but you will realize that clinging to certainty is often the first step to disappointment.

The Indian tennis icon Sania Mirza's life is a vivid reminder that when life turns a page, it often brings in characters you never expected. From being India's tennis sensation to navigating a very public marriage, facing online scrutiny, and later embracing motherhood, coaching and advocacy, her journey has never followed a linear path. People she probably thought would stay didn't. In interviews, she has often spoken about the comfort she found in unexpected friendships—women she barely knew earlier, mentors she once competed against, and strangers who reminded her of her worth when public opinion was unkind. Her life shows that while the stage may change, the script is never quite done.

Unlike the earlier lesson, which reminds you not to expect permanence, this one asks you not to fear transition. Because while change can hurt, it can also heal. The most precious kindness often comes from the most unexpected people. The next chapter may not have the old faces, but it might just offer new meaning.

If you think life is a straightforward journey, be ready to be proved wrong. The plot twists are what make it worth the read.

20

Crises show people's true character.

That is what we see in crises or tough moments.

I have had abundant experience. Almost all through my life.

A crisis often becomes the clearest lens through which people's true character comes through. I remember a particularly challenging phase when I faced a serious personal setback. People who I thought would stand by me, simply vanished, while others—some I hadn't even considered close—stepped up in ways that left a lasting impression on my mind. One friend in particular, who I'd known mostly in passing, pitched in with quiet, steady support. No questions asked. Finally, it's moments like these that reveal people's deepest values and priorities. These experiences, though painful, are almost like a blessing in disguise, for they provide a glimpse into who truly deserves a place in your life.

That same clarity can be observed on a national stage too. During the early waves of the COVID-19 pandemic, while systems faltered and institutions struggled, actor Sonu Sood became an unlikely yet extraordinary symbol of leadership in crisis. He arranged transport for stranded migrant workers, provided shelter and meals, and later even built platforms for jobs and education.

What stood out wasn't just the scale of his efforts, but the deeply personal way in which he showed up: taking phone calls from strangers in need of help, responding to pleas on social media, tracking journeys. At a time when even well-meaning people kept a distance, he was in the thick of it all.

That's what a crisis does—it reveals, with sharp and sometimes painful clarity, who people really are. It shows you who will stand still while everything else is in motion. Who disappears, who deflects, who steps up—and how. And just as it reveals others, it also teaches you something about yourself: your tolerance, your strength, your blind spots. Crises strip away the decorative layers of life, leaving behind only what is real.

What you learn from these moments stays with you. The faces that quietly turn away, and those that quietly remain, become etched in memory.

21

Let it go. Don't be negative.

It is simply not worth it. Truly.

The resentment, the simmering grudge, the mental reruns of what was said to you, or done to you—they only deplete you. You may think you're justified in holding on, but you're the one who pays the price.

It drains your energy. It distorts your perspective. It makes you look bitter. And worse, it chips away at relationships that might still be worth salvaging.

Each of us has a scar. That one memory from years ago that still stings. An old boss who belittled you. A former friend who betrayed your trust. A family member whose words still echo in your head.

But you cannot stay stuck there. Carrying those memories like emotional luggage weighs you down far more than it hurts those who inflicted them. The damage is internal, corrosive and quiet. Like a poison tree, it grows inside, twisting your sense of self and making you relive pain that should have long been behind you.

The truth is, people say and do things out of their own limitations. Their own fears, insecurities, or blindness. That does not make it okay, but it does make it easier to stop taking it personally. Sometimes, you just have to conclude that they did not know how to behave.

And move on. Not because they deserve it, but because you do.

Deepika Padukone, one of India's most admired contemporary actors, has exemplified this lesson in ways both public and personal. At the peak of her success, she was subjected to harsh scrutiny, cruel trolling, and even malicious speculation around her mental health. She could have responded with bitterness or anger, but instead, she chose grace. Not only did she open up about her struggles with depression—breaking a massive stigma in Indian society—but she also channelled her pain into purpose. Through her foundation, she began advocating for mental wellness, helping others feel less alone. She didn't lash out. She didn't turn bitter. She transformed negativity into a platform for healing, not just for herself, but for thousands of others. That's what it means to let go, but in active choice.

Forgiveness is not about forgetting what happened. It's about refusing to let that memory control your mood, your mind, or your milestones. The more you hold on to resentment, the more power you give to the one who hurt you. When you let go, you reclaim that power.

Staying away from negativity isn't about being naive. It's about preserving your energy for what truly matters—growth, peace, and purposeful relationships. In a world already full of noise, don't be an echo of your past wounds. Be a voice of your present strength.

Let it go. And walk lighter into the rest of your life.

22

It's okay to be embarrassed.

It truly is.

Embracing those cringeworthy, red-faced moments can be strangely liberating. The moment you realize that you are a little like Teflon—able to let things slide off without sticking—life becomes instantly brighter. Embarrassment loses its sting when you stop letting it define you. Laugh it off, shrug it off, and carry on. Once you do so, you'll notice that those moments that felt unbearable in the past now add colour to your life and even bring you closer to others. After all, everyone loves a good story about tenacity, and nothing speaks more than being able to rise, smiling, from life's awkward moments.

Many famous figures have embraced embarrassment as a stepping stone to growth, showing us that it's perfectly okay to feel embarrassed and face it. Take Jennifer Lawrence, for instance. Known for her candid personality, she famously stumbled at the Oscars while climbing the stairs to receive her Best Actress award. Instead of letting it overwhelm her, she laughed it off, even making a joke about it afterward.

Talk show host Ellen DeGeneres often pokes fun at herself, saying that her most embarrassing moments have been the best teachers, and finest material for comedy in her life.

Shah Rukh Khan often recounts how he struggled in his early acting days, feeling embarrassed by his lack of knowledge about the film industry. Yet, he used these moments to learn and grow, building a career on his authenticity and self-confidence.

Each of these icons shows that when you accept embarrassment as part of the journey, you not only learn to laugh at yourself but also become more relatable.

23

You will not be understood every time.

Even family and friends and colleagues might misjudge you.

Or misinterpret your words and actions.

It's fine. In a world shaped by diverse experiences, perspectives and personal biases, being misunderstood is inevitable. Socially, expecting to be understood always, often leads to frustration when people—including family, friends, or colleagues—fail to see things from our perspective.

Cultural differences and generational gaps further amplify the chances of misjudgements or misinterpretation. This is particularly common in professional settings, where communication styles vary, and in personal relationships, where emotional nuances often remain unspoken. Accepting that one cannot be universally understood fosters emotional steadiness. It shifts the focus from seeking validation to staying authentic and learning to navigate relationships with empathy, clarity, and grace.

Author J.K. Rowling experienced this life lesson when her early Harry Potter drafts were misunderstood by publishers as being 'too niche' or 'not marketable enough'. Instead of letting these misjudgements deter her, she stayed true to her vision, ultimately creating one of the most beloved series in literary history.

Indian environmentalist and innovator Sonam Wangchuk faced scepticism when introducing his ideas for solar-powered schools in Ladakh. Many dismissed his efforts as impractical. Yet, he persevered, knowing his work spoke louder than misinterpretations.

A more offbeat example is British explorer Bear Grylls, whose survival techniques have been criticized as extreme or theatrical. Yet, Grylls sees these responses as inevitable and focuses on inspiring self-reliance and grit.

These examples remind us that misunderstandings and mistrust often accompany individual uniqueness; the real challenge is to remain committed to our convictions despite all odds.

24

Have a hobby. Or many.

Be passionate about hobbies.

They keep you sane, even when the world thinks you are not.

Many famous personalities have found solace and balance through their hobbies, often pursuits quite removed from their professional lives.

Mahendra Singh Dhoni, one of India's most celebrated cricketers, has always had a passion for motorcycles. His collection is extensive, but more importantly, his enthusiasm for riding and maintaining them has been a grounding influence amid the intense demands of cricket and celebrityhood.

Bill Gates, despite his high-powered career in technology, finds immense joy in reading. Known for devouring book after book, Gates has shared how reading offers him a welcome retreat from the hectic life of business, and philanthropy.

Dhoni's and Gates' hobbies are not mere pastimes; they are anchors that help maintain their sense of self, keeping them grounded when the world around them is anything but.

25

Enjoy silence.

Silence is underrated.

With so much noise, conversationally and philosophically, one needs to build a practice of silence and solitude.

No wonder most of us enjoy our time on the pot!

Silence is profoundly underrated in our society. It's often equated with awkwardness, embarrassment, or even discomfort, rather than being embraced as a powerful personal technique. We have become so accustomed to filling every moment with sound—be it with the television at home, music in the car, or headphones at the gym—that true silence feels almost unnatural. Even in situations as brief as an elevator ride or while being placed on hold during a call, piped music replaces silence. We dread 'awkward silences' when meeting someone new, unsure of what to say.

Silence can be a sanctuary, a way to centre ourselves and let our thoughts settle. When embraced rather than avoided, silence can be a potent source of calm and clarity in an increasingly noisy world.

Many famous personalities have recognized the power of silence as a tool for maintaining focus, cultivating fortitude, and even building influence.

Actor Keanu Reeves, known for his private, reserved nature, often speaks about how silence helps him stay grounded in an industry full of noise. Rather than rushing to respond or make statements, he uses his silence to reflect, helping himself navigate fame with humility and grace.

In the world of business, even musician David Bowie, who was often bold in his art, was known to withdraw into silence when creating music—an essential step he felt that allowed him to reconnect with his inner voice and refine his unique style. For such influential figures, silence has always been far more than the absence of sound; it has been a deliberate, powerful practice that has shaped their approach to life and work.

26

Live your life, and with honesty.

> Don't live on behalf of your parents or your friends.
>
> Live your *own* life. Every moment of it.
>
> But with your values intact.

Honesty is the true test of strength of character.

For much of my life, I considered myself 'honest enough'—I stayed honest as long as things were going my way. But when life threw challenges my way, I found myself looking at truth as a part, not the whole.

I still remember, early in my career, being asked to 'adjust' a report so it would pass a review more smoothly. The change wouldn't have hurt anyone directly, and it would have saved me weeks of extra work. For a moment, I was tempted—everyone around me said it was harmless. But that night, I couldn't sleep. I realized that if I agreed, I would be living someone else's version of my life, not mine. I refused to make the change, knowing it might cost me favour with my boss. Strangely, it didn't make life harder in the long run; it made me feel lighter. That one decision became a touchstone for how I approached every ethical choice thereafter.

Over time, I learnt the hard way that honesty isn't conditional; there is no 'right way' to do the wrong thing. You're either honest or you're not. I understood that real honesty requires unwavering determination. It's your commitment to living by your values, regardless of the circumstances. Real honesty means committing to truth in its entirety, not choosing only those bits that suit the moment. Living honestly requires strength. Not only the big choices but the small, daily decisions that you make truly define who you are.

27

Live within your means.

But seek quality within what you can afford.
Don't let your wants become your needs.
It is those needs that make you needy, and tamper with your moral compass.

In a world increasingly driven by consumerism and the pressure to showcase status, living within one's means is both a personal discipline and a societal necessity. Cultures worldwide, including in India, often grapple with the dual forces of tradition—emphasizing frugality and balance—and modern aspirations, which push individuals toward material excess.

This is not about austerity for its own sake, nor about glorifying minimalism as the only virtuous path. It is about alignment, ensuring that your lifestyle reflects both your values and your resources, rather than the demands of external validation. Don't let your wants disguise themselves as needs, for it is those artificial needs that make you needy, and tempt you to compromise your moral compass.

Financial stability and moral integrity are deeply intertwined; when individuals stretch themselves to maintain appearances or fulfil fleeting desires, they risk compromising their long-term security and even their ethics. Living within one's means fosters self-respect and independence while allowing individuals to seek quality in what truly matters, whether in experiences, relationships, or investments in self-growth. This balance is crucial not only for an individual's wellbeing but also for a sustainable and equitable society.

Warren Buffett, one of the wealthiest individuals in the world, famously lived in the same modest home he bought in 1958, demonstrating his commitment to living within his means despite his immense wealth. This discipline has allowed him to channel resources into meaningful ventures, like philanthropy, rather than indulging in luxuries.

In India, Dr A.P.J. Abdul Kalam was known for his simple lifestyle despite his fame and influence. He never let material aspirations overshadow his values, choosing to focus on his work and contributions to society.

The example of Indian tea-seller-turned-social-entrepreneur Laxman Rao shows how quality can be pursued within one's means. He sold tea to fund his self-published books, showcasing that one can balance practicality with passion without falling prey to unnecessary excesses. These individuals underscore the value of aligning one's lifestyle with one's personal values and resources, thereby ensuring a life of dignity and purpose.

28

Be accountable for what you do or don't.

That's what I think the 'sixth sense' of humans is all about. It's the instinct to stand up and say, 'Yes, this was mine to do, and I own the outcome,' whether good or bad. If we shy away from being accountable, we are, by this logic, not even living fully as humans.

Accountability is more than admitting fault—it is the conscious choice to act on what you've learnt. When you own your role in a failure, you confront the truth without excuses. That clarity becomes the starting point for change: you see exactly what went wrong, what you could have done differently, and what you can do next. Without ownership, you circle the same mistakes again and again because you've never examined them closely enough.

Owning your part also builds trust. People will forgive a misstep far more quickly if they believe you're taking responsibility and working to make it right. And the act of sitting with the discomfort-guilt, embarrassment, frustration-without running from it builds the emotional muscle you'll need for bigger challenges ahead.

An excellent example of a sportsman who embraced accountability, even after a significant failure, is Michael

Jordan. Though he is celebrated today as one of the greatest basketball players in history, Jordan faced a major setback early in life when he was left out of his high school basketball team. It was a moment that could have crushed his spirit. Instead, Jordan took responsibility for putting in the effort required, and used it as fuel to work even harder. His accountability for his own progress, rather than blaming others or his circumstances, pushed him to train relentlessly. He later famously said, 'I've missed more than 9,000 shots in my career. I've lost almost 300 games. Twenty-six times, I've been trusted to take the game-winning shot and missed. I've failed over and over and over again in my life. And that is why I succeed.' Jordan's acceptance of failure, and accountability for his efforts, became the bedrock of his legendary work ethic, ultimately transforming him into an icon.

29

Treat yourself to a luxury as a reward.

Once in a while.

I did when I achieved a career goal I had set for myself before I turned forty.

I rarely used my car, as I was travelling much more outside of Mumbai. But that car was a reminder of my journey over the past twenty-five years.

In these times, even fresh air and good-quality natural resources like water and oxygen seem to come at a premium.

In societies that often swing between thrift and extravagance, I have come to believe there is a sweet spot—one where you can live with discipline yet still allow yourself the joy of a well-earned treat. In a culture like ours, where modesty has long been seen as virtue, a luxury often carries the weight of guilt unless it is tethered to a milestone. I have found that when you link a reward to something you've worked hard for, it deepens your respect for both the effort and the reward.

It isn't a break from living within your means, but rather an affirmation of it, because you choose the moment, you choose the indulgence, and you choose it without debt or pretence. In that choice lies a kind of dignity, a reminder that self-discipline and self-appreciation can sit comfortably at the same table. The world will always tempt us with instant gratification, but the occasional, mindful indulgence—be it a holiday, a fine meal, or a treasured possession—can become a quiet celebration of progress, a way of marking life's milestones without losing sight of what matters.

Jeff Bezos, founder of Amazon, exemplifies this lesson with his acquisition of The Washington Post. While it may seem extravagant, he saw it as a reward for his journey and an opportunity to contribute to the world of journalism—an area he deeply admires.
Indian badminton champion P.V. Sindhu, after years of disciplined training and victories, has treated herself to indulgences like designer handbags and fine dining, using them as tokens of her achievements.

Another fine example is the Indian chef and entrepreneur Ranveer Brar, who after successfully launching a new restaurant, goes on culinary tours to explore gourmet experiences.

30

You can't plan everything.

The staunch planner that I am, every aspect of my life had once been meticulously slotted into my calendar, down to the last hour and minute. Every goal, every step, even every pause, was orchestrated to fall perfectly into place. But life, as it often does, had other ideas. Suddenly, there were unexpected detours, and surprises that were far from pleasant, and changes I couldn't control. At first, it was frustrating. Plans unravelled, schedules meant little, and my carefully laid paths became winding roads. Yet, through this, I learnt some of the most valuable lessons of all: perseverance, flexibility, and the peace that comes from surrendering control. I learnt that life doesn't run on anyone's schedule but its own, and the beauty is in how we respond to the unexpected. Today, I still plan, but I leave room for life's spontaneity, understanding that sometimes the unplanned brings the greatest growth. No hard feelings—just a newfound respect for the art of letting go.

Many well-known figures, including Indian business icons, have learnt the power of adapting when life doesn't go as planned. Ratan Tata, for instance, faced an unexpected challenge when Tata Motors acquired Jaguar Land Rover (JLR). Despite strategic plans, the

2008 global financial crisis hit soon after, nearly derailing the acquisition. Rather than adhering rigidly to their original plans, Tata and his team pivoted, doubling down on innovation, which ultimately transformed JLR into a profitable entity.

Similarly, Apple's journey under Steve Jobs offers a powerful reminder that even the most visionary leaders can't predict every turn. When Jobs returned to Apple in 1997, the company was weeks away from bankruptcy. The original plan was to stabilize its core computing business and slowly rebuild. But the rapid evolution of technology and changing consumer needs demanded bolder, faster moves. The iPod, iPhone, and iPad weren't on the company's early recovery roadmap—yet they became the very innovations that redefined not just Apple, but entire industries. Jobs once remarked, 'You can't connect the dots looking forward; you can only connect them looking backwards.' It's a truth that underscores how openness to the unexpected can lead to results far beyond even our most detailed plans.

31

Your spouse—life's greatest co-pilot in change

That, for me, is the kindest and the best lesson life taught me.

Probably that's why they say marriages are made in heaven.

But whether you have heaven in your earthly marriage probably depends on your karmic balance.

There are some who are not that lucky. For whatever reason, the marriage falls apart. No marriage is perfect. Just as no one is.

Of all the roles a spouse plays, perhaps the most underestimated is that of a change manager. Life rarely stays still, and marriage is the one partnership that must weather every shift, big and small. Your spouse is the person who sees every version of you—the dreamer, the worrier, the achiever, the one quietly hanging on—and adapts alongside you. They absorb the shocks, share the pivots, and sometimes take the wheel when you cannot.

Marriages are not perfect, because people aren't. Some unions don't last, and the reasons are as varied as life itself. But when trust and unconditional love form the foundation, marriage becomes more than companionship—it becomes a living, breathing partnership where both are mutual change managers. You grow together, you stumble together, and you learn to make space for each other in the innermost corners of your life.

A beautiful example of this is former Indian cricket captain Anil Kumble and his wife Chethana. When Kumble's career demanded long absences, intense training schedules, and the highs and lows of public scrutiny, Chethana provided stability, perspective, and a grounding presence. She adapted to his demanding professional life, while he, in turn, embraced her priorities and commitments. Together, they navigated career transitions, personal challenges, and public life with quiet dignity—showing that the strongest marriages are those where both partners evolve together.

A successful marriage is not about avoiding change; it is about navigating it hand in hand. The resilience, empathy and flexibility you show one another become your greatest tools for survival and joy. And in those moments when life takes an unexpected turn, it is often your spouse who reminds you that while the route may be different, the journey is still worth taking—especially together.

32

You and your spouse don't need to have the same hobbies or interests.

As long as your values are the same, it's okay.

Having hobbies or interests different from those of your spouse can be a source of richness rather than rift, as long as you both are aligned in your core values. When a relationship is grounded in shared principles—mutual respect, honesty, a common vision for family and life, etc.—it allows each partner the space to pursue their passions freely, without feeling pressured to match the other's interests. Divergent hobbies can even enhance a relationship by keeping things fresh and bringing new perspectives into shared conversations. Imagine the thrill of discovering new facets of each other through these differences, rather than expecting a mirror image.

Many well-known figures illustrate how shared values are more important in relationships than identical hobbies or interests. Former President of the United States Barack Obama and former first lady Michelle Obama make a notable example: despite differing interests—Barack being deeply engaged in basketball and reading, while Michelle enjoys yoga, gardening, and community outreach—their strong, shared commitment to family, integrity and public service has firmly cemented their marriage.

In India, actors Riteish Deshmukh and Genelia D'Souza have often shared how they maintain their individual passions—Riteish is passionate about architecture and design, while Genelia is a fitness enthusiast and loves cooking—yet their partnership is founded on common values of humility, mutual respect, and family first. These shared values have allowed them to nurture each other's unique interests without conflict, proving that while hobbies may differ, shared values are what truly strengthen a relationship.

33

When your spouse is upset, just stay silent.

That's like holding onto a strong pillar when the storm is raging.

But be genuine with your affection and care.

In most situations, words only worsen the reason why your spouse is upset, even if it's not your fault.

And don't even attempt to decipher the reason why your spouse is upset. (S)he will tell you, more often when you least expect it, and after much time has passed.

Silence, paired with genuine care, is not passivity but strength. It allows emotions to settle and creates space for clarity, showing that sometimes love speaks loudest in the quiet moments. This following anecdote underscores this powerful truth.

Staying silent when your spouse is upset is a lesson that resonates universally, even with well-known figures. Sudha Murthy, renowned author and wife of N.R. Narayana Murthy, once shared in an interview how their relationship thrives on mutual understanding and patience. She recounted a moment early in their marriage when she was upset about Murthy prioritizing work over family time. Instead of trying to argue or explain his position, Murthy chose to listen silently and offer gentle reassurance through his actions rather than words. In time, her frustration melted away, and she found herself explaining her feelings to him on her own terms.

34

People are passages.

People happen. They arrive in your life without warning, stay for a while, sometimes for years, sometimes for days, and then one day they leave. Some departures are gentle and mutual, others abrupt and painful.

The truth is, neither the joy of arrival nor the ache of parting is permanent. You learn to meet each with the same calm, because clinging to either will only weigh you down.

In recent decades, our social structures have shifted dramatically. The joint family gave way to the nuclear family, and now many live alone, navigating demanding careers and personal ambitions. High-pressure jobs, relocations, and the constant churn of urban life make relationships more transient than ever. Friendships can form in an instant over a coffee break and dissolve just as quickly when circumstances change. Accepting this reality doesn't make you cold—it frees you to appreciate people for the season they are with you, instead of resenting them for the season they are not.

Each person who passes through your life brings a gift—sometimes it is joy, sometimes it is a lesson, sometimes it is simply the reminder that you can connect at all. If you focus on the quality of the connection rather than its duration, you can hold on to the value without holding on to the person.

Former President of the United States Barack Obama learnt to accept the transience of relationships during his political career. In his memoirs, he reflects on how the demands of public life often distanced him from old friends and even family at times. Rather than allowing these changes to embitter him, he embraced the fact that people come and go, thus recognizing that life has seasons, and some connections are meant to evolve or fade. This acceptance has allowed him to cherish his present relationships deeply, without clinging to the past.

35

Ego is overrated.

Vanity is overdone.
Sanity is key.

From the Bhagavad Gita to the sayings of saints and sages, our scriptures remind us that ego and vanity cloud our judgement, limit our growth, and distance us from others. Ego traps us in a cycle of self-importance, while vanity draws us toward the superficial, causing us to lose touch with our inner selves. Both are distractions from the real purpose of life—cultivating humility, clarity, and peace of mind. The concept of *santosh* or contentment, often emphasized in Indian philosophy, speaks to the deeper need for inner calm and sanity.

In this context, sanity means seeing life with clarity, holding your balance, and standing steady through its inevitable challenges. Sanity is about valuing your actions, character, and relationships over material accomplishments or the need for external validation. True wisdom, as our spiritual teachers remind us, lies in finding peace within and letting go of the ego—a path that brings far more fulfilment than the fleeting illusions of vanity and ego.

Indian cricket legend Sachin Tendulkar, despite his extraordinary achievements, has always remained grounded and gracious, letting his work on the field speak for itself rather than succumbing to ego. He often credited his success to his coaches, family, and teammates, exemplifying humility in the face of global adulation.

Bollywood superstar Shah Rukh Khan has remarked on how he chooses to laugh at himself and not take his own celebrity status too seriously, understanding that ego is a trap.

These individuals demonstrate that shedding one's ego opens doors to deeper connections, growth, and provides a sense of purpose, reminding us that success shines brighter when it is divested of self-importance.

36

Children are your investment in sanity.

Hold on to every moment you can spend with them.

There will come a time when they will not want you around, and when you will not want them around either.

If you don't have children of your own, make friends with other children you know.

And remember, if you are not genuine, they will see through it.

Children have a way of bringing clarity to our otherwise complicated adult lives. Their questions make us think in straightforward terms, their reactions are unfiltered, and their priorities are often refreshingly simple. Spending time with them can strip away the excess noise of daily pressures, reminding us of what is essential and worth our attention. In their company, we often regain perspective, finding a steadier, calmer view of the world and our place in it.

That children are your investment in sanity resonates deeply with many renowned personalities who find grounding and purpose through their relationships with their children. Former Indian cricket captain Rahul Dravid often speaks about how spending time with his son provides a sense of balance and normalcy amid the pressures of his public life.

Global icon Michelle Obama has often shared how her daughters, Sasha and Malia, anchor her in moments of uncertainty, reminding her of life's more important priorities.

37

Remember and pay back every act of loyalty and service extended to you and your family.

One of life's most profound lessons is to remember and honour those who have stood by you and your family in difficult times. Due to their loyalty and support, these people—friends, mentors, colleagues, even community members—who have offered kindness, guidance, or a helping hand during tough times, have become an integral part of your life. Their loyalty is a gift, a quiet strength that deserves recognition and gratitude.

Expressing gratitude for their support, whether by returning a favour, offering help in their time of need, or by simply showing genuine appreciation, or paying it forward, is a way of completing the circle of kindness and respect.

It reflects our values, and our commitment to nurturing meaningful connections. Remembering and reciprocating acts of loyalty not only strengthens these bonds but also fosters a spirit of gratitude and integrity that we carry forward. It also builds a formidable strength of character.

Ratan Tata's response to the 2008 Mumbai attacks

on the Taj Mahal Palace Hotel stands as a profound example of remembering and standing by those who have shown loyalty and service. After the devastating incident, Tata didn't just focus on restoring the hotel; his concern extended to every person impacted by the tragedy. He ensured that the families of the hotel staff who lost their lives were taken care of, offering full compensation, covering their education expenses, and providing medical care to their dependents. What truly stands out is how, going beyond his employees, Tata supported street vendors, rickshaw drivers, and even pedestrians who were affected during the attack, ensuring they received aid. His empathetic leadership and unwavering commitment to those connected to the hotel reflect a deep sense of gratitude and responsibility, showing that true leadership is about standing by everyone who has contributed to your life, no matter how directly or indirectly. This act of humanity is still remembered as a hallmark of his values.

38

Pass goodness forward.

Never ask what someone did for you. If you can offer a simple helpful gesture for someone, without even being asked to, just do it. Not for boasting rights. But for the simply joy of it.

Trust me, it is delightful.

But after that act, don't think of it. Move on.

And if you can't help out in a situation, please do not to give a lecture on how to handle it.

Kailash Satyarthi, the Nobel Peace Prize laureate, has spent decades rescuing children from child labour, slavery and trafficking, often at great personal risk. What is remarkable is that his efforts were never transactional—he didn't rescue children to gain fame or favour but out of a deep conviction to create a better world. Satyarthi once shared how, after liberating a group of children, one of them expressed the desire to help others once grown up. That child went on to establish a grassroots organization for educating children in rural India. Satyarthi's willingness to give without expectation created a ripple effect of kindness, proving that when you pass goodness forward, it often inspires others to do the same.

39

Have a sense of humour.

It relieves stress.
It keeps you sane.
It makes you humble.
It makes life tolerable.

A sense of humour is also a quiet teacher. It shows you how to laugh at yourself, how to ease tension in a room, and how to see the lighter side of a setback. In moments when words fail or tempers flare, a well-timed smile or quip can dissolve barriers faster than logic or persuasion ever could.

But again, a sense of humour is underrated, and actually is in short supply.

The late Dr A.P.J. Abdul Kalam—known for his humility and wisdom—often used humour as a bridge to connect with people. Once, during a live interaction, a young student asked Dr Kalam a seemingly awkward question: 'Why do you always comb your hair backwards?' Dr Kalam, instead of being taken aback, laughed and replied with a twinkle in his eye, 'It's because it's the easiest way! No effort needed, and the wind can do the rest.' His light-hearted response not only diffused the awkwardness but also showcased his ability to turn an awkward moment into one filled with warmth and relatability.

Richard Branson, the British entrepreneur, has often used his sense of humour to navigate challenges. From dressing as a flight attendant for a friendly bet with his competitor to laughing at his own business failures, he shows that humour can humanize even the most tense situations.

40

Never take a decision when you are angry, or hungry.

It is human tendency to let emotions and physical discomfort cloud judgement. Anger, often fuelled by heightened emotions, narrows our perspective, making us prone to taking impulsive decisions that we may regret later. Likewise, hunger triggers irritability and impatience, diminishing our capacity for rational thought. Across societies, such situations are resolved through the practice of pausing before reacting—taking time to meditate in Indic practices, or counting till ten before responding as Thomas Jefferson had suggested, or the ritual of breaking bread together to ease tension. Societies thrive on harmony and thoughtful leadership, and this lesson reminds us to prioritize clarity and calm over impulsive reactions, thereby ensuring that decisions are fair, considered, and beneficial in the long run.

Legendary Indian cricketer Mahendra Singh Dhoni is renowned for his calm demeanour and impeccable decision-making skills, especially under pressure. Dhoni has frequently spoken about staying composed during high-stakes moments, emphasizing the importance of not letting emotions dictate his actions. He attributes his success as a captain to his ability to think clearly and rationally, even in the most challenging situations, by first calming his mind before making crucial decisions.

Michelle Obama has shared similar wisdom in her reflections. During her tenure as first lady, she faced numerous challenges but always ensured she addressed them with a clear and level head. In her memoir *Becoming* (2018), she talks about how she and Barack Obama adopted the practice of 'sleeping on it' before making major decisions, especially during moments of tension or exhaustion.

41

The tone of the voice matters.

The tone you use to say something has an effect—positive or negative, intended or unintended.

Use it wisely.

Cultivate the right tone.

No book teaches you this, but your powers of observation would certainly help with this life lesson.

A harsh, high-pitched tone or speaking loudly as if you are bossing around, can put people off. Thereafter, you can't expect them to be kind and understanding. The tone you choose is often remembered long after your words are forgotten. It can either open a door or quietly close it. In professional settings, it shapes perceptions of competence and empathy; in personal relationships, it can turn an ordinary exchange into a moment of comfort or conflict. Tone is not just sound; it's the emotional signature of your presence.

Renowned Indian spiritual leader Dada Vaswani often spoke about the transformative power of a gentle tone. Known for being soft-spoken, his ability to convey profound wisdom in a calm, soothing voice won over people of all backgrounds. He believed that the tone of one's voice carries as much meaning as the words themselves and often demonstrated how a calm demeanour could diffuse tension.

The late Steve Irwin, the beloved Australian wildlife expert, used an enthusiastic yet comforting tone to share his passion for conservation, even when discussing dangerous animals. His tone made the wild seem approachable, and inspired millions to care about nature. Both leaders exemplify how choosing the right tone fosters connection, trust, and understanding, proving that the tone is an unspoken yet powerful language of its own.

42

Physical fitness is your friend.

Work on it consciously.

There's nothing cold or cynical in saying this: while friends will often send warm wishes and help in small ways when you're unwell, sustained care usually falls to those closest to you. That reality isn't meant to shame anyone and it simply reminds us that investing in our health is an act of responsibility, independence and kindness to those who love us.

Work on your fitness every single day—not just through exercise, but by cultivating habits that bring composure, steady your mind, and help you make better choices about what you eat and drink.

When I went through a bout of poor health, it was a reminder that life happens, despite all your planning. But the positive desire to wade through is what makes your recovery better and deeper. Again, this is a lesson I relive every day for my health and wellbeing.

Many renowned personalities have shown how crucial physical fitness is in supporting not only their careers but also their overall wellbeing. Akshay Kumar, the Bollywood actor, despite his busy schedule, is an early riser who maintains a strict fitness regime that includes martial arts and functional training. He credits his longevity and consistency in a demanding industry to his dedication to fitness, proving that staying active is an invaluable asset.

The late Steve Jobs, though known more for his tech innovations, valued physical wellness, often taking long, reflective walks and practising mindfulness to stay sharp and resilient.

Tennis star Serena Williams has also pushed the boundaries of athleticism and strength through disciplined training routines even post-motherhood, thereby proving that physical fitness can empower and energize us, regardless of life's demands.

Each of these individuals highlights the fact that prioritizing physical fitness builds a foundation for both personal and professional endurance, allowing one to tackle challenges with vitality and fortitude.

43

Cooking is a life skill.

You don't need to compete in MasterChef, or serve up a fine-dining fare.

Just learn to make 10 dishes with tasty nutritious seasonal produce that you can have as a meal, every day. That's worth half the fortune that you will earn through your life.

Cooking is one of the few life skills that directly impacts your health, finances, and independence every single day. Knowing how to make a few wholesome meals means you are never entirely dependent on restaurants, takeaways, or someone else's schedule. It sharpens planning skills—choosing ingredients, balancing nutrition, avoiding waste, and builds an instinct for making the most of what's available. In moments of transition, whether moving cities, facing long work hours, or caring for family, this skill quietly sustains you in ways money alone cannot.

Indian actress and fitness icon Shilpa Shetty is a great example of someone who has embraced cooking as a life skill. Known for her love of clean eating and nutritious meals, she often shares simple, wholesome recipes that emphasize seasonal produce and balanced nutrition. She believes that cooking is not just a way of staying healthy but also a creative and mindful activity that connects you with your body and culture.

Global actor Hugh Jackman, admired for his down-to-earth nature, has often showcased his passion for cooking at home. Jackman credits his cooking skills for keeping him connected with his family and allowing him to unwind after hectic schedules.

Another example is chef-turned-entrepreneur Sanjeev Kapoor, who has always championed the idea that cooking isn't just a skill for professionals—it's essential for everyone. He has encouraged people across India to learn the basics of cooking to lead a healthier, more self-reliant life.

All three personalities highlight that cooking isn't about culinary showmanship; it's about self-reliance, health, and creating moments of connection.

44

Memories are important.

You have your childhood memories and stories, even though others may not understand their significance, or even relate to why you feel what you feel about them.

You have your favourite songs from your growing-up years that will fill you with joy or nostalgia, depending on your mood.

Enjoy such memories that each of us as human beings carry around for a lifetime. Cling on to your memories without forcing them on others.

Memories may not define you. But surely, they bring sanity to your life. Memories often serve as anchors in a fast-changing world. They become a sanctuary, offering clarity and creativity in turbulent times. They serve as a private space of comfort, joy, and even quiet introspection, enabling us to stay connected to our roots and to find a sense of stability amid life's chaos. No matter how insignificant they may seem to others, Memories carry a profound meaning for each of us.

Memories are also an unseen compass. They can guide choices, shape values, and remind you of lessons you might otherwise forget. Many renowned personalities have drawn strength and solace from their past.

Indian cricket legend Rahul Dravid, for example,

has spoken about how revisiting childhood memories of playing cricket on the streets of Bangalore with friends grounds him during moments of stress.

Acclaimed author Maya Angelou would often revisit the stories and songs from her childhood in Stamps, Arkansas, to draw inspiration for her writings and speeches.

45

Life is lonely.

No one who is happy or rich is likely to confess it, for they are rarely without company. Yet life often proves the opposite—there can be moments when the room is full, the laughter loud, and still a quiet loneliness hums beneath it all. It is a paradox both fiction and reality have long understood, and one worth recognizing early.

No one really cares about your pain and worries, beyond their own tolerance level and their mental bandwidth.

So simply accept that your emotions are just your own.

The notion that 'life is lonely' speaks to a deep societal reality often obscured by the noise of social connections, achievements, and appearances. In modern life, where relationships can sometimes feel transactional or surface-level, loneliness is not about physical isolation but emotional disconnect. The paradox lies in the fact that one can be surrounded by people, even celebrated, yet feel profoundly lonely—an experience amplified in a world driven by individualism and performance. Society rarely offers space for vulnerability, as people's capacity for empathy is often restricted by their own struggles and limited bandwidth. This lesson is a reminder to accept that your inner emotions are ultimately yours to process and own. True peace comes not from expecting others to share your burdens but from finding strength and clarity within, while seeking meaningful connections that transcend the superficial.

Indian screenwriter, poet and lyricist Javed Akhtar has often spoken about the loneliness that accompanies success, especially in creative fields. Despite his acclaim and in spite of being surrounded by admirers, he has acknowledged moments when personal pain and introspection have been his own to bear.

The globally celebrated chef and travel documentarian, Anthony Bourdain, shared in his writings how loneliness can pervade even the most glamorous lives. Constantly surrounded by people on his travels, he often felt disconnected, highlighting that true companionship is rare.

46

Life is unfair.

Life is tough.
But then, that's why we were born as human beings, and not as any other beings.
Face life as it comes.
Stay well.
Stay good.
Think good.
Do good.
Life will eventually balance out.

The idea that *life is unfair* resonates universally, transcending cultures and social strata. Societies often condition individuals to expect fairness, yet real-life experiences seldom align with this ideal. Economic disparity, social inequality and unforeseen challenges remind us that life doesn't distribute opportunities or outcomes evenly. However, the human capacity for resilience, compassion and action makes life's struggles bearable and meaningful. Cultures worldwide emphasize the importance of 'karma' or 'reaping what you sow', suggesting that even amidst apparent unfairness, goodness and effort can lead to an eventual balance. This perspective is vital in shaping an optimistic, proactive mindset, encouraging people to persist rather than succumb to cynicism or despair.

Jane Goodall, the renowned primatologist, faced ridicule early in her career for her unconventional methods and lack of formal scientific training. Instead of lamenting life's unfairness, she persevered, eventually revolutionizing primatology and global conservation efforts.

Closer to home, rural self-taught doctor Padma Shri awardee Harekala Hajabba used his modest earnings as an orange seller to fund a school in his village, undeterred by systemic inequities.

Their stories highlight that while life may seem unfair, persistence, goodness and purpose can create profound, positive change.

47

It is okay to accept that you don't remember.

Many a time, at work or in my personal life, I have met people who I didn't remember from prior interactions.

I learnt that people could make a mountain out of a molehill in such scenarios. But it's fine to say graciously and with humility, 'Sorry I am not able to place you. My fault.'

Forgetting is part of being human, not a sign of indifference. What matters is the grace with which you handle it. When you acknowledge it openly, you not only disarm any potential awkwardness but also signal that the person in front of you matters enough for you to try again.

This time around, think of it as a reset moment to know that individual better.

Acknowledging that you don't remember someone or something can be a powerful gesture of humility and authenticity. Dr A.P.J. Abdul Kalam once spoke about the importance of approaching people with honesty. In his interactions, if he couldn't recall someone's name, he would apologize graciously, redirecting the focus on making the current moment meaningful rather than dwelling on memory lapses.

48

Teach.

Each one of us should teach. I am glad that this journey for me started very early in my life.

Go back to your school, college, wherever.

But teach what you know.

That's one way to strengthen what you know, and to realize what you really don't know but thought you did.

Teaching has little to do with titles and designations—it's a deeply human act that fosters meaningful exchange, humility and introspection, and creates an impact. Whether it's mentoring a young colleague, guiding your children, or giving back to your alma mater, teaching reminds you that knowledge truly multiplies when shared.

So, just teach.

Dr A.P.J. Abdul Kalam, also known as the 'Missile Man of India', spent significant time teaching students even after holding the highest office in India. He believed that educating young minds was his way of shaping the future.

Globally, Bill Gates has stepped into the role of educator, sharing insights on technology, climate change, and global health through his books, interviews, and online platforms.

49

Spiritual quotient is key.

Learn to be guided by the spiritual side of wisdom.

Don't be carried away by mumbo jumbo.

You will get a teacher or master or guru who will guide you. Just that they don't need to be clothed in saffron, ochre or white, nor do they need to come with a social tag. If you really want a guide, life has a way of making it happen.

Spiritual quotient (SQ) is the foundation of inner balance and clarity in an increasingly chaotic world. Unlike intelligence quotient (IQ) or emotional quotient (EQ), spiritual quotient focuses on a deeper connection with oneself and the universe, enabling an individual to navigate life's challenges with resilience and grace.

Rajinikanth, one of India's most iconic actors, is a living testament to the power of spiritual quotient. Despite his immense fame, and the adulation he enjoys, he has always remained grounded, attributing his calm demeanour to his spiritual practices. Known for his simple lifestyle, Rajinikanth often retreats to the Himalayas to meditate and reflect, seeking clarity and purpose away from the limelight. His spiritual grounding has helped him navigate both personal and professional challenges with grace. Whether it's handling criticism, the pressures of superstardom, or even health setbacks, Rajinikanth's inner calm has always been his strength. His journey teaches us that while material success and public adoration are transient, spiritual quotient provides lasting peace and clarity in life.

50

Your child is not your own.

Kahlil Gibran said: 'Your children are not your children [...] They come through you but not from you.'

This is not just poetry, but a reminder of the spiritual truth that we are born of biological parents, yet we are children of the cosmos. In that sense, every life is touched by divinity. Our role is to care for the next generation, but without clinging to worldly attachments that hold them back from realizing their potential.

Life has a way of nurturing them. If we give them values, and teach them the importance of moral unrighteousness, the rest will be the doing of their own karma.

To my girls, you have great potential to be good humans. That's the highest one can strive to achieve, beyond riches, fame, success, and the like. However, earn everything through care, hard work and legal means while being honest and morally upright.

As much as we nurture, guide, and love our children, they are individuals with their own identities, dreams, and paths to carve. The role of a parent is not to impose but to support—to be a gardener who tends to the soil, not a sculptor chiselling a predetermined shape.

Hence, parenting in today's world requires letting

go of ownership and embracing mentorship. The joy of parenting lies not in control but in witnessing your children grow into who they are meant to be, knowing their lives are their own masterpiece, shaped by their choices and experiences.

This philosophy found quiet expression in the way J.R.D. Tata led. He did not see the younger generation or his employees as possessions to be moulded, but as individuals with their own unfolding potential. His way was to guide without suffocating, to set high standards without dictating every step, trusting that when you give people space, they will often surprise you by rising above your expectations. He believed that true growth comes not from constant oversight, but from the freedom to make choices and learn from them. In doing so, he nurtured a culture where responsibility was embraced, and excellence was pursued not out of fear, but from within.

51

Chase excellence. Perfection is a mirage.

Perfection, being subjective and often elusive, can hinder creativity and discourage effort, while the pursuit of excellence focuses on consistent improvement and doing the best that one is capable of.

Jackie Chan, the legendary martial artist, actor, and filmmaker, embodies the life lesson of chasing excellence rather than perfection. Known for his unparalleled work ethic and dedication, Jackie has never been fixated on creating flawless performances but instead, strives to push boundaries and improve with every project. In his early Hollywood days, Jackie faced criticism for his strong accent and unfamiliar action style. Yet, rather than trying to perfect his English or change his craft to fit into a mould, he focused on excelling in what made him unique: blending martial arts with humour and breathtaking stunts. His dedication is evident in how he often performs his own stunts, accepting that minor mishaps are part of the process, but they ultimately contribute to something extraordinary. An anecdote from his career highlights this pursuit of excellence. During the filming of *Police Story* (1985), Jackie insisted on performing a dangerous stunt where he slid down a pole wrapped in lights. Though he sustained severe burn injuries, his determination to give the best shot resulted in a scene hailed as one of the greatest stunts in cinema history. Jackie's career shows that striving for excellence, learning from setbacks, and being true to one's craft is far more impactful than chasing an elusive idea of perfection.

The same principle applies beyond film sets—in classrooms, offices, laboratories, and homes. Excellence is not about erasing every flaw; it is about showing up fully, doing the work with integrity, and pushing the boundary of one's own ability. Perfection chases an illusion that belongs to someone else's standard; excellence builds a legacy that is uniquely yours.

52

Value your time.

If you don't, no one else will.

You will then end up busy, but without any meaningful context or relevance to your existence.

Your job doesn't pay for your existence; it simply leases hours from your life, hours that are finite, irreplaceable currency. Time is the only asset that never appreciates, only depletes, and once spent, no paycheque can buy it back. Spend it with intent, choosing carefully who and what occupies it, for each interaction is either an honoured guest or an uninvited burden. Your hours are like water in a clay pot—once poured out, they seep into the earth forever. So guard them fiercely and pour them where they will nourish life, not drain it.

Choose carefully who and what occupies your time—each interaction is either an honoured guest or an uninvited burden.

What value do they bring in return? Does it justify what you're sacrificing?

Your time is limited, a shrinking treasure with each passing moment. Treat it as a garden, not a dumping ground. Cultivate it with care, remove what chokes its growth, and fill it only with what you wish to see flourish. Nurture it into something that fills you with pride, not regret. Build, diversify, elevate its worth. Invest in yourself and watch your life flourish.

Indian business tycoon N.R. Narayana Murthy has long emphasized the importance of valuing time. Known for his disciplined approach, he maintains strict adherence to punctuality and prioritizes meaningful work over unnecessary distractions. Murthy once recounted how, during Infosys' early days, he would meticulously plan every minute of his day, ensuring that even his interactions brought value to the company's vision.

Anya Taylor-Joy, the young and talented actress known for *The Queen's Gambit* (2020), is an excellent example of someone who values time. Despite her rising stardom, she is known for being extremely selective with her roles and how she spends her time. Anya has often spoken about how she avoids the chaos of constant socializing or distractions that come with fame, choosing instead to focus on her craft and personal growth. She credits this disciplined approach for enabling her to deliver powerful performances and stay grounded in an industry known for its overwhelming demands. Her story is a reminder that valuing time isn't just about professional success—it's also about creating space for what truly matters to you.

53

Value the ones who show up

'We should catch up. It's been pending.'

'Let's meet soon.'

A set of common phrases used to indicate interest but hardly sincere, serving as delightful examples of how people bandy these around to express their non-existent warmth.

I have learnt from my own and others' experiences that if people really mean what they say, they would take the initiative to 'catch up'.

You will realize soon enough that you are better off with a select few people you can relate to, and want to spend time with.

Don't chase people. If something is not meant to be, it simply won't. The truth is, if someone genuinely wants to be in your life—whether for friendship, collaboration, or support—they will make the effort. They will send the first message, fix a date, rearrange a schedule. It's not about being cynical, but about recognizing that time and attention are the truest currencies of care. You save yourself much heartache when you stop chasing those who repeatedly signal interest but never follow through.

This is not only a lesson in relationships; it is also one in energy management. You cannot force reciprocity, just as you cannot plant seeds in barren soil and expect a harvest. The people who matter will prove themselves not with words, but with presence. Invest in them.

Serena Williams offers a clear example of living this principle. Over her decades in tennis, she learnt to narrow her circle to those who genuinely had her back—not just during victories, but also in injury, recovery, and public criticism. By choosing to pour her energy into those who consistently showed up, Serena protected her mental bandwidth and extended her career. Her journey is a reminder that life's richest relationships are not the ones that sound good in theory, but the ones that stand the test of time, inconvenience, and silence.

Don't waste energy chasing people who drift in and out as per their convenience. Cherish those who are already here—showing up, even quietly, in ways that truly matter.

54

Not all relationships are for keeps.

Some break off soon.
Some come off the rails after a time.
For reasons, at times not too clear.
Just go with the flow.

Even friendships, marriages, family relationships, professional relationships change. Simply because the context changes for all the individuals involved. Relationships evolve because the individuals involved evolve. Contexts change, priorities shift, circumstances alter, and the dynamics of once-close ties may weaken. Friends might drift apart as their life stages differ; marriages may become strained when mutual goals or values no longer align. Even family and professional bonds can falter under the weight of unspoken expectations or changing realities. Accepting this truth isn't about apathy, but about understanding that every relationship serves its purpose for a certain time. Letting go gracefully allows you to cherish what was, while creating space for newer, more meaningful connections.

Some relationships end quickly, like doors shutting in a gust of wind. Others unravel slowly, like fabric fraying thread by thread. The reasons may be clear—distance, conflict, shifting priorities or maddeningly vague, leaving you to navigate unanswered questions.

Relationships change because people change: life stages differ, values evolve, and circumstances shift. Friendships, marriages, family ties, even long-standing professional bonds can falter under unspoken expectations or diverging paths. Accepting this isn't about indifference, but about recognizing that every connection has its own season. Letting go gracefully allows you to value what was, without clinging to what can no longer be. It's a quiet strength-one that cherishes the shared moments while making space for relationships yet to come.

Human behaviour in relationships often reflects deep-seated needs: the need for validation, control, even self-preservation, among others. When these needs no longer align, bonds become strained under the weight of unspoken truths. Accepting this impermanence is liberating—it allows us to cherish the moments shared with people without clinging to the hope of their continuity. It teaches us that not all relationships are meant to last, and that's okay. Every connection, however brief, serves a purpose—as a lesson, a memory, or simply as a moment of shared humanity.

A role model for this truth is Roger Federer. Throughout his career, Federer formed close bonds with coaches, training partners and fellow players, but he never clung when it was time to part ways. Roger Federer has worked with several coaches throughout his career. Key figures include Peter Lundgren, Tony Roche, Paul Annacone, Stefan Edberg, Severin Lüthi, and Ivan Ljubičić.

He always spoke with gratitude, acknowledging that each partnership had served its purpose in his growth. His enduring friendship with Rafael Nadal, despite fierce rivalry, shows that some relationships adapt and thrive, while others fade naturally and that both outcomes are part of life's rhythm.

55

Blood is not thicker than water.

Don't confuse metaphors and relationships.

Every relationship needs constant effort to make it work.

Don't take relationships lightly.

I have taken quite a few lightly, and paid the price for it. I have also seen how sometimes lineage is hyped. Lineage does not necessarily make relationships work. Intent—and genuinely working on them—does.

From a societal perspective, the phrase *blood is not thicker than water* highlights a profound truth: relationships, whether familial or otherwise, are not automatically strong—they require continuous effort to thrive. In traditional societies, family ties are often assumed to be unbreakable, but the modern world reveals that even these bonds can falter without care and communication. Friendships, professional alliances, and chosen families often surpass biological relationships in emotional depth because they are nurtured with intent. This shift reflects a broader societal reality: people are increasingly seeking relationships that are built on shared values, respect, and mutual effort, rather than defaulting to those dictated by blood. While familial connections hold cultural significance, valuing effort over entitlement ensures healthier, more meaningful relationships across all spheres of life.

Meaningful relationships are cultivated through mutual respect and effort, not just through shared DNA, underscoring the idea that connections built on trust and care are often stronger than those of lineage.

That blood is not thicker than water finds resonance in the life of the football icon Cristiano Ronaldo. Despite his fame, Ronaldo has often spoken about how trust and effort matter more than biological ties. He shares a close bond with his inner circle—many of whom are not related by blood—because they have consistently stood by him through triumphs and challenges.

Closer home, Indian actor Manoj Bajpayee has highlighted how friendships he formed during his theatre days became his true family, as they supported him during his early years of struggle in Mumbai.

56

The tongue is key.

If you can control your tongue, it is the best discipline.

The tongue is what gets us into trouble most often.

What we speak.

What we eat.

The tongue, often seen as a small part of the body, wields immense power—constructive and destructive. What we say has the ability to inspire, heal, and connect, but it can also harm, offend, or escalate conflicts when used recklessly. Similarly, what we eat reflects discipline and self-control, affecting our physical and mental wellbeing. Controlling the tongue requires mindfulness and patience, as it involves resisting the urge to react impulsively or indulge excessively. By mastering the tongue, we cultivate harmony within ourselves and with others, ensuring that our words and habits align with our values and intentions. In essence, the tongue becomes a tool for peace and balance when wielded wisely.

Globally, the Dalai Lama embodies this principle by emphasizing the importance of kind and truthful speech. Even when discussing contentious topics like Tibet's sovereignty, his words remain gentle, showing that the tongue, when controlled, becomes a tool for wisdom and peace. In a world where public figures often get embroiled in controversies due to offhand remarks, Rajinikanth has consistently avoided unnecessary conflicts. During political discussions or debates about his career choices, he chooses his words carefully, often opting for silence or a simple, impactful statement. For instance, when questioned about sensitive political matters, he has often replied with dignity and wisdom, refusing to stoke controversy while still expressing his stance calmly. His ability to measure his words, even in the most provocative situations, showcases not only his discipline but also his deep understanding of how powerful and lasting words can be.

57

Pay for quality.

Be it food, experiences or lessons. Or the talent or skills you want.

You are valuing your own wellbeing, growth, and happiness.

Good food fuels your body, giving you the energy and health to pursue your dreams. Memorable experiences enrich your life, offering new perspectives and joy that stay with you for long. Paying for quality lessons or skills, whether professional or personal, accelerates your growth and brings out the best in you, enabling you to accomplish your goals with confidence. Similarly, paying for top talent or skills, whether in a team or in your personal network, can make a remarkable difference. Surrounding yourself with skilled, passionate people elevates your own standards and opens up greater possibilities.

Choosing quality is a declaration that you believe in your own worth. It isn't about luxury; it's about sustainability, respect, and care for what truly matters. Compromising on quality often costs more in the long run, whether in the form of regret, repairs, or lost opportunities. Quality food saves you from health issues; quality lessons sharpen your mind, and quality relationships enrich your life. By valuing quality, you create a ripple effect—what you receive is a reflection of what you give. It's not about spending extravagantly but about aligning your resources with your aspirations and values.

Indian businessman Harsh Mariwala, the founder of Marico, built a consumer goods empire by focusing on premium, quality-driven products. In his journey, Mariwala consistently advocated investing in high-quality inputs, whether it was raw materials for his products or hiring top talent for his team.

58

Keep seeking answers.

There are times when you don't find answers.

That's life.

Don't break your head, or lose heart over not finding answers.

That does not mean you give up.

From a young age, society conditions us to expect quick resolutions—instant feedback, immediate results, and fast solutions. Yet, life is rarely so accommodating. Relationships falter, careers stall, and challenges arise that defy simple answers. In these moments, society's relentless pace can make us feel left behind, isolated, or even inadequate. However, the true value lies not in immediate clarity but in the process of seeking, learning, and evolving.

Stephen Hawking exemplified the essence of continuing to seek answers. Diagnosed with a debilitating illness at a young age, he faced more questions than answers about his future. Yet, instead of succumbing to despair, Hawking channelled his energy into unravelling the mysteries of the universe. His groundbreaking work on black holes and cosmology wasn't born from immediate clarity but from persistent inquiry despite life's uncertainties.

Indian innovator Sonam Wangchuk, known for revolutionizing education and sustainability in Ladakh, faced numerous roadblocks when trying to adapt modern solutions to traditional contexts. Instead of giving up, he kept experimenting—seeking answers that blended technology with local needs.

Both their stories remind us that life often presents only questions, but the journey to seek answers, with patience and resilience, leads to growth, innovation, and a deeper understanding of life's lessons.

59

Not everyone needs to be simple.

You need all kinds of individuals, with varying lifestyles (as long as they can afford it), to be around. If you haven't ever observed this, it is precisely what makes the economy work.

Don't pass judgement on someone just because they look glamorous or are spendthrifts—their context and intent are different from yours. Do not try to be them.

In a society as diverse as ours, the idea that *not everyone needs to be simple* reflects the richness of human expression and economic dynamics. Individuals with varying lifestyles—whether rooted in simplicity or opulence—play a vital role in shaping cultural and economic landscapes. The so-called 'glamorous' lifestyles, often misunderstood as vanity or excess, fuel industries like fashion, entertainment, and tourism, creating jobs and opportunities for countless others. At the same time, those who choose minimalist lives set examples of sustainability and resourcefulness. Passing judgement on someone's lifestyle without understanding their context or intent only limits our perspective. The truth is, society thrives on this diversity, as this diversity fosters innovation, drives consumption, and reflects the multifaceted aspirations of people. The key is not to emulate others but to coexist and respect the choices that make the world more vibrant and interconnected.

Manish Arora, with his flamboyant designs and vivid use of colours, built a brand that celebrates extravagance and unapologetic individuality. Often criticized for being 'too loud' or 'over the top', he stayed true to his vision, which created opportunities for artisans, drove creativity in Indian couture, and made him a globally recognized name.

Kim Kardashian, often perceived as a symbol of glamour and indulgence, has turned her lifestyle into a billion-dollar business empire through ventures in beauty, fashion, and media.

Both individuals challenge the notion that simplicity equals virtue, showing that different lifestyles can coexist and contribute uniquely to the economy and society. Their stories remind us not to pass judgement on others' choices but to appreciate the diversity that fuels progress and innovation.

60

What if I don't learn more all the time?

A feeling that drives me on.
To seek.
To ask.
To be awkward.
To learn.
To learn from anyone who has something to offer, even if they offer it without intention or concern.

The societal aspect of a mindset driven by the question 'What if I don't learn more all the time?' highlights the value of intellectual humility and perpetual growth. In a world where knowledge evolves rapidly, the willingness to embrace awkwardness and seek understanding from any source—regardless of its status or intent—becomes a critical skill. It challenges societal norms of expertise being tied to titles or formal qualifications, fostering an environment where learning is seen as a shared human endeavour. This mindset not only empowers individuals to grow beyond their limitations but also enriches communities by encouraging diverse perspectives and collaborative innovation. Ultimately, it reflects a culture where curiosity fuels both personal progress and collective advancement.

Amit Trivedi, the celebrated Indian music composer, has often spoken about how his journey in music is driven by a relentless thirst for learning. Known for blending genres and creating unique sounds, Trivedi didn't start with any formal training in many of the musical styles he later mastered. He sought to learn from diverse sources—mentors, fellow musicians, or even by observing the rhythms of everyday life.

Elon Musk, a name synonymous with innovation, credits his success to his willingness to ask questions and learn, even in fields he initially knew little about, like rocket science. Both personalities embody the essence of being highly curious, and unabashedly open to growth. Their journeys remind us that learning is a lifelong pursuit, and that openness to insights from any source—even when they arrive coloured by bias or shaped by a specific agenda, can still spark personal growth and continual reinvention.

61

There is a lesson to be learnt from everyone.

I was pompous enough to believe that only the educated could offer lessons. I learnt that education is not a substitute for *learning*.

Life's lessons abound in places where you hardly expect them.

Be it from a roadside tea seller.

Or a bus conductor.

Or your workplace junior.

Or a person you meet on a flight.

Societally, we often associate learning with formal education and authority, creating a bias that knowledge flows only from those with credentials or status. This mindset limits our ability to see the wisdom in everyday interactions and people. For instance, the tea seller at a roadside stall might embody resilience, balancing a difficult life with a smile, while a bus conductor might demonstrate impeccable discipline amidst chaos. These moments of humility remind us that learning is not confined to classrooms or books. Individually, our biases often make us overlook the contributions of those we perceive as 'ordinary,' failing to recognize that lived experiences, resourcefulness, and emotional intelligence offer lessons no degree can provide. When we let go of these biases, we open ourselves to a world where wisdom emerges from the most unexpected places, enriching us in ways traditional education cannot. Life's lessons often come from those outside the spotlight, proving that life's greatest teachers can often be the ones who are least expected to be.

Sports and politics often provide great examples of learning from unexpected sources. Former Indian cricket captain Kapil Dev has shared how he learnt critical life lessons from a young ground staff member during his early days in cricket. The worker's dedication and cheerful attitude in maintaining the pitch, despite long hours and limited resources, taught him the value of persistence and gratitude.

In politics, Barack Obama frequently acknowledged the wisdom he gained from conversations with everyday citizens during his campaigns. He spoke of a farmer in Iowa who, through his simple yet poignant words, shaped Obama's understanding of grit in the face of economic hardship.

P.V. Sindhu, India's badminton star, once mentioned how observing young players in training reminded her of the importance of humility and of going back to the basics, no matter how accomplished one becomes.

62

When words fail, let kindness speak.

Especially when you face others' emotions, you may not know how to respond.
Or what to say or do.
Being kind may be the answer.

From a societal perspective, emotions often come with cultural expectations that can make them even more challenging to navigate. In many cultures, especially those with deeply ingrained hierarchies or collectivist values, displaying or responding to emotions openly can be deemed inappropriate. Individuals may fear saying the wrong thing, appearing insensitive, or exposing their own vulnerabilities. This is compounded by personality traits such as introversion, insecurity, or the inability to process intense feelings.

The cultural challenge lies in finding the balance between empathy and maintaining composure, especially in environments where emotions are often suppressed or seen as a sign of weakness. In such moments, kindness becomes the universal response—a way to bridge cultural divides, ease discomfort, and connect authentically. Kindness doesn't demand perfect words or actions but offers a simple, humane way to show care when emotions are overwhelming.

Kindness is not a weakness but a strength, enabling us to navigate others' overwhelming emotions with grace and compassion. It reminds us that when words fail, a kind gesture or a willing ear can go a long way.

When ISRO's Chandrayaan-2 mission faced a setback in 2019, ISRO Chairman K. Sivan broke down after the lander lost communication during its descent. Prime Minister Narendra Modi, present at the ISRO headquarters, demonstrated a deeply empathetic and human response. As Sivan struggled with visible emotions, Modi offered him a heartfelt embrace, reassuring him and the entire team that setbacks were stepping stones to success. His words, 'The effort was worth it, and the nation is proud of you,' conveyed a powerful message—failure is a moment in the journey, not the destination.

On the global stage, Hollywood actor Keanu Reeves, often lauded for his humility, has been seen comforting grieving fans by sharing his own experiences of loss, offering words of understanding rather than solutions.

63

Don't compare. But set a benchmark.

There is a difference.

If you compare, then it becomes individual-led and emotional at a point, perhaps even with some negativity.

But if you set a benchmark, you will know where you stand in a competitive world. Then you can work at bettering yourself.

Comparison often feeds emotions like envy, insecurity, or unwarranted pride, narrowing the focus to individual rivalries while draining mental energy. It creates an atmosphere of judgement, where achievements and failures are measured against personal biases rather than broader standards. Benchmarking, on the other hand, is rooted in growth and objectivity. It encourages individuals to measure their progress against established norms, fostering a spirit of self-improvement without diminishing anyone. In a societal context, benchmarking promotes a collective aspiration for excellence—whether in education, innovation or a profession—without pitting individuals against one another unnecessarily. For example, countries that benchmark their policies or industries against global standards progress faster by focusing on improvements rather than dwelling on disparities. On a human level, benchmarking is empowering—it lets you focus on growth and goal-setting, steering clear of the emotional pitfalls of comparison. It's about progress, not perfection.

In the world of competitive cycling, Lance Armstrong's story, while controversial, offers a glimpse into the power of benchmarking. Before his fall from grace, Armstrong revolutionized the sport by benchmarking his performance against physiological data and his competitors' racing strategies, focusing on metrics rather than getting emotionally entangled with individual rivalries.

Closer to home, E. Sreedharan, India's 'Metro Man', exemplified this mindset in infrastructure projects. Instead of comparing India's rail systems with other countries, he benchmarked it against global engineering and operational standards, ensuring projects like the Delhi Metro met international standards of excellence.

Both examples demonstrate that benchmarking encourages growth and excellence without the distraction of comparison. It allows individuals and organizations to focus on measurable improvements rather than getting bogged down in subjective rivalries. This approach is a powerful tool for staying grounded and achieving meaningful progress.

64

Dream.

Dream on.
Dream big.
That's what makes life enjoyable.

That's why, I realized, fiction as a genre works well. Dreaming is humanity's most transformative trait—a spark that fuels progress, innovation, and joy. Dreams, whether personal or collective, provide a sense of purpose that transcends the mundane. That is why fiction as a genre captivates so many; it creates worlds where possibilities are boundless and where imagination reigns supreme. Societally, dreams play a dual role: they inspire change-makers to reimagine the world and to offer the average person a temporary escape from the daily struggles.

Yet, dreaming big isn't just about escapism; it's a cultural commentary on hope. In a world of inequalities and challenges, dreaming allows individuals to envision better futures, reminding us that growth begins with belief in the improbable. Fiction mirrors this spirit, showing us that no reality exists without first being dreamed into existence.

Paulo Coelho, the globally celebrated author of *The Alchemist* (1988), faced countless rejections and struggled with societal expectations before achieving literary fame. Yet, he held onto his dream of wanting to become a writer, pouring his soul into a manuscript that would later inspire millions to chase their own dreams.

Indian entrepreneur and restaurateur Prafull Billore, popularly known as MBA Chaiwala, dared to dream beyond societal norms. From dropping out of a prestigious MBA programme to setting up a roadside tea stall, he envisioned building a tea brand that resonated with India's youth. His dream transformed into a reality, proving that even the most unconventional aspirations can lead to extraordinary success.

65

Reading is a necessity. It is not a hobby.

Read regularly and on a variety of topics.
Read even those topics that won't help you in your career and life right away.
Read as much as you can.
For knowledge is a friend.

In a society increasingly driven by rapid consumption of bite-sized information, the act of reading deeply and widely is no longer a luxury—it is a developmental necessity. Reading fosters critical thinking, broadens cultural horizons, and helps individuals transcend the limitations of their immediate environment. In the Indian context, where oral traditions have long coexisted with a rich literary heritage, the habit of reading offers a bridge between preserving traditional knowledge and embracing global perspectives.

Socially, reading fosters empathy by exposing readers to lives and ideas vastly different from their own. Culturally, it counters the growing trend of digital distractions by encouraging sustained focus and intellectual curiosity. Developmentally, reading on diverse topics nurtures adaptability and problem-solving skills, critical in an ever-evolving world. Ultimately, it anchors individuals in knowledge, empowering them to engage meaningfully with their communities and the larger world.

Reading as a necessity has been exemplified by individuals like Dr A.P.J. Abdul Kalam, who credited much of his visionary thinking to the breadth of his reading. From engineering journals to philosophy and poetry, his diverse reading allowed him to bridge science with humanity.

J.K. Rowling, before becoming famous with her Harry Potter books, was an avid reader of classics, mythology, and obscure works. Her voracious reading helped her create a richly layered fictional world, offering lessons in resilience and imagination.

Sudha Murty, who is both an engineer and a prolific author, has spoken of how reading beyond her field—from Kannada literature to Western novels—shaped her empathy and storytelling.

66

There is a lot of goodness around.

If only you look, search and listen.

I have seen that people whom I thought were aloof, powerful, powerless, not friendly and distant, step up to help. Without being asked.

In that, life has a way of bringing you to those who matter, when it matters. When you want it with your heart.

Call it prayer. Call it meditation. Call it blessing.

Throughout my life, goodness has found me—sometimes in moments of need, sometimes as an unexpected gift, often far more than I could ever reciprocate with. It is not the absence of gratitude, but the realization that some acts of kindness are too profound to repay, except by passing them forward. Such people and goodness make the world a better place.

In a world often overshadowed by negativity in news, politics, or social media, the innate goodness of people can go unnoticed. Socially, we are conditioned to focus on self-preservation, leading to us overlooking acts of kindness and altruism around us. However, culturally, many traditions stress the idea of collective goodwill—be it through community service, rituals of gratitude, or the simple practice of helping one another. The challenge lies in recognizing these moments of goodness, especially in fast-paced urban settings where interactions often feel transactional. The importance of this lesson is profound: it reminds us to keep faith in humanity and to foster a sense of gratitude and belief in the unseen support around us, even when we might not immediately notice it.

Globally renowned chef José Andrés epitomizes this lesson with his World Central Kitchen initiative. During disasters, Andrés has served millions of meals to those in need, showing that even amidst chaos, human kindness flourishes.

Indian forest conservationist Jadav Payeng, often referred to as the 'Forest Man of India', spent decades single-handedly planting trees on a barren island, not for recognition but out of belief in the greater good.

A more unexpected example is that of Swiss explorer and scientist Bertrand Piccard, who found unexpected support from local communities during his solar-powered flight around the world. People he had never met provided shelter, resources and encouragement, reinforcing his belief in goodness.

These stories highlight how, if we stay receptive and look beyond the obvious, life reveals its hidden reservoir of kindness, waiting to be acknowledged and cherished.

67

Leadership is an earned privilege.

Not a birthright.
So work for it.
Act with care. Be kind. Leading is a responsibility.

Leadership, across societies, has long been influenced by power structures like lineage, socioeconomic status, or traditional hierarchies. However, modern culture increasingly challenges the notion of leadership as an inherited right. Democracies, start-ups, and social movements have shown that true leadership is not bestowed but earned through trust, vision, and action. This shift reflects a growing cultural emphasis on meritocracy and accountability.

In this context, leadership is seen not as a position of dominance but as a responsibility to inspire and uplift others. Societies now value leaders who demonstrate empathy, inclusiveness, and the willingness to serve, recognizing that the privilege to lead must be earned, nurtured, and constantly validated by actions.

Malala Yousafzai, despite her young age, exemplifies how leadership is earned through resilience and advocacy. After surviving a brutal attack, she used her voice to lead a global movement for girls' education, not because of her background but because of her determination and sense of purpose.

Ratan Tata's leadership of the Tata Group wasn't rooted in privilege but in his ability to prioritize ethics, philanthropy, and long-term vision over immediate gains.

A less conventional example is Jane Goodall, whose quiet leadership in primatology and conservation was built on years of fieldwork and deep respect for the environment.

These individuals remind us that leadership is not an entitlement; it is a privilege earned through consistent actions, care for others, and the willingness to shoulder responsibilities for collective progress. In my own journey, I have found that the most enduring authority comes not from titles or positions, but from the quiet respect of those who know you have their trust at heart.

68

Mentoring others is an accountability that comes from trust.

Maintain that trust and do not abuse that privilege.

It is a fine way of sharing what life has given you.

Mentorship, deeply embedded in cultural practices worldwide, is often seen as a bridge between generations, skills, and experiences. Societies depend on mentors to guide individuals, shaping careers and values. However, this relationship thrives on mutual trust.

Abuse of this trust can lead to exploitation, bias, or the withholding of opportunities, eroding the cultural significance of mentorship. In a world where professional networks and collaborations are growing, the accountability of mentors has never been more crucial.

A good mentor does not impose but empowers, passing on wisdom without personal gain. This trust-based relationship ensures that knowledge, insights, and values are transferred with care, ensuring continuity and fostering a culture of mutual growth and respect.

Michelle Obama has often credited her mentors for shaping her perspective and career, but she also shares how she consciously mentors young women, particularly from underprivileged communities, without overshadowing their individuality.

N.R. Narayana Murthy believes in empowering the next generation of leaders by guiding them without micromanaging anything, thereby ensuring they learn accountability and decision-making.

Offbeat examples include Chef Massimo Bottura, who mentors young chefs in his kitchens, encouraging creativity while instilling discipline.

These leaders understand that mentorship is not about control but about sharing knowledge, fostering independence, and preserving the sacred trust that comes with guiding someone's journey.

69

Native intelligence

Don't brush it aside.

It's the best thing you can learn from.

Native intelligence is a reservoir of wisdom rooted in centuries of lived experience, tradition, and cultural practices. It represents the understanding of local environments, ecosystems, and social dynamics that formal education often overlooks. In today's world, where modern science and globalized systems dominate the discourse, native intelligence is often dismissed as unscientific or obsolete.

Yet, this wisdom is essential in fields such as sustainable farming, natural medicine, and community living. Recognizing native intelligence not only preserves cultural heritage but also offers practical solutions to global challenges like climate change and resource management. By blending modern science with native knowledge, societies can achieve holistic progress that respects both innovation and tradition.

We willingly overlook the native intelligence of *haldi-doodh* (turmeric milk) as a drink with anti-inflammatory and anti-oxidant properties, yet happily pay for dollar-priced turmeric lattés—because apparently, native intelligence tastes better when rebranded.

The late Dr A.P.J. Abdul Kalam, during his interactions with rural communities in India, emphasized learning from traditional farming techniques to address food security challenges.

Vandana Shiva, a prominent environmentalist, incorporates native seed preservation methods, rooted in indigenous knowledge, to advocate for sustainable agriculture.

A standout example is Babu Varghese, the ecotourism pioneer from Kerala, who reimagined the traditional kettuvallam rice boats into modern, flood-resilient houseboats, launching the first tourist backwater cruises and transforming them into an enduring symbol of Kerala's hospitality and culture.

In rural Rajasthan, water conservation expert Rajendra Singh revived traditional water-harvesting systems like *johads*, showcasing how native intelligence can solve modern crises.

70

Never be jealous of others.

Surely you don't know the problems they face.

You are entitled to the benefits of your own karma. And your own efforts and thoughts.

Jealousy, often a product of societal competition and cultural conditioning, thrives in environments that celebrate material success and superficial achievements. Social media and modern lifestyles have magnified this tendency, presenting curated glimpses of others' lives that often exclude the struggles behind the scenes. However, jealousy blinds individuals to their unique journey and undermines their own efforts and blessings. By focusing on personal growth, and understanding that every life comes with unseen challenges, one can replace envy with empathy. Cultivating gratitude for one's circumstances fosters inner peace and creates a society that values collective wellbeing over relentless competition.

Renowned naturalist and broadcaster Sir David Attenborough, despite his unparalleled achievements, has often spoken about finding fulfilment in personal purpose rather than comparing himself to peers.

In the Indian context, Jadav Payeng chose to focus on his singular mission of creating a forest in Assam rather than feeling envious of others with more resources or recognition.

Another outstanding example is the anonymous street artist Banksy, who channels creative energy into impactful art rather than seeking fame or competing with the mainstream art world.

Each of these individuals exemplifies the power of appreciating their own journey without envy, trusting that true fulfilment lies in authentic self-expression and effort.

71

Respect even those who doubt you.

Life will inevitably surround you with people who may lack self-awareness, understanding, or competence. They might be strangers, colleagues, critics—or even your own sibling or boss. Education, position and power are no antidotes to such behaviour. But don't treat them any lesser than you would treat yourself.

Instead of building hierarchies of worth based on perceived intelligence or behaviour, choose to engage with dignity and patience. This doesn't mean agreeing with them or enabling poor decisions, it means maintaining your own character regardless of theirs. Accepting that some situations and people cannot be changed equips you to navigate both professional and personal relationships with calm, clarity, and empathy.

Jadav Payeng was often ridiculed when he began planting trees on Majuli Island. Many thought his efforts were foolish, yet he responded with kindness and let his work speak for itself. Albert Einstein, too, was known for his respectful engagement with critics, even those who dismissed his theories as nonsense. Their examples remind us that kindness towards doubters and detractors is not a sign of weakness, but of inner strength—the quiet assurance that one's path is defined by integrity, not by the opinions of others.

72

Have reliable and trusted advisors.

> Be hundred per cent honest with them.
> Good-quality advice and good advisors are rare.
> Cherish their trust and advice.

In today's fast-paced world, where expertise and timely advice are essential for navigating complex life choices, having a trusted set of professionals at hand—doctors, legal advisors, financial planners, tax experts, among others—is crucial. Whether it's managing health, ensuring financial stability, or navigating legal complexities, the right advice can make all the difference. In many cultures, the emphasis is on building long-term relationships with such experts, where trust is paramount.

These advisors not only provide expert guidance but also help bring peace of mind, since you have the assurance about making informed decisions in critical areas of your life. Their insights help you avoid costly mistakes, whether in personal finance management, navigating health crises, or ensuring legal compliance. In a rapidly evolving, knowledge-driven world, where decision-making is increasingly becoming complex, a reliable advisor acts as a safeguard, offering clarity in a sea of choices. Moreover, fostering long-term relationships with these professionals allows for tailored advice based on a deep understanding of your unique circumstances, goals, and values. This continuity strengthens trust, making them more than just service providers—they become key partners in your personal and professional growth.

Being honest with them, respecting their time and regularly paying their fees reflect the value people place on their expertise. Ultimately, investing in quality professional advice ensures a smoother, more secure journey through life's challenges.

Indra Nooyi, the former CEO of PepsiCo, exemplifies the power of surrounding oneself with trusted advisors and valuing their counsel. Throughout her remarkable career, she consistently sought honest feedback from a close circle of mentors and experts, recognizing that no leader, no matter how talented, can succeed alone. Nooyi's openness to diverse perspectives and her respect for expert advice helped her navigate complex business challenges and drive transformative growth.

73

Anger is self-consuming.

I learnt that after nearly four decades of living.
After it had already consumed much of feelings, emotions, relationships and more.
So, don't be angry.
It's not worth you. Yes, I mean *you.*
Just give up anger. Stay away from it.
You are worth much more. You have more potential to achieve.
More dreams to chase.

Anger is a universal human emotion, but its implications differ across cultures and societies. In many traditions, such as Indian philosophy and Eastern practices, anger is seen as a fire that consumes not only relationships but also the self. Modern psychology agrees, highlighting the destructive effects of unresolved anger on mental and physical health. Socially, anger often exacerbates conflicts and fractures communities, making dialogue and progress more challenging. In a world driven by high-stress environments and fast-paced living, learning to manage anger becomes crucial for personal growth and societal harmony. By choosing calm over rage, individuals can focus their energy on productive and transformative pursuits, realizing their true potential and contributing positively to society.

The Dalai Lama, despite facing the exile of his people and the destruction of Tibetan culture, advocates compassion over anger, seeing forgiveness as a path to inner peace.

Dr A.P.J. Abdul Kalam was known for his calm demeanour even in the face of criticism and setbacks. He believed that anger distracted from the pursuit of greater goals, choosing instead to focus on innovation and education.

Self-taught Indian artist Nek Chand, creator of the Rock Garden of Chandigarh, transformed his frustration over urban waste into an iconic art space.

Such pathbreakers exemplify how abandoning anger can redirect energy toward creating lasting legacies and achieving dreams.

74

Travel.

As much as possible.
As much as you can afford.
Be frugal if you want. But travel.
It is one of the best teachers.
But be open to learning about new places, people, societies, culture, etc.

Travel has always been a profound means of broadening horizons, fostering understanding, and dismantling biases. In a world divided by cultural and social barriers, travelling allows individuals to connect with diverse communities, witness unfamiliar traditions, and appreciate the similarities that bind humanity. It is an experiential education that teaches tolerance, adaptability, and humility. Beyond leisure, travel deepens one's understanding of history, art, cuisine, and the socio-economic fabric of various societies. The cultural exchange that travel enables also strengthens bonds and breaks down stereotypes, making it a critical tool in creating a more empathetic and inclusive global society.

Maya Angelou, the celebrated American author, once said that travelling makes you realize 'how much we all have in common'.

Indian photographer Raghu Rai's travels to remote

Indian villages have not only enriched his art but also allowed him to showcase the beauty and resilience of rural life to the world.

Another fine example is Meenakshi Gupta, the founder of the NGO Goonj, whose travels across India's hinterland inspired her to bridge the urban-rural divide through innovative solutions.

Even Swedish climate activist Greta Thunberg, known for her eco-conscious travel choices, uses every journey as a way to promote sustainability and learn from communities facing environmental challenges.

Each of these individuals embodies the belief that travel is more than a luxury—it is a teacher, a connector, and a means of personal and societal transformation.

75

Age and maturity have no correlation.

Age is overrated.
One can be mature even at twenty.
Likewise, being fifty does not necessarily mean one has tact and maturity.
The ability to learn from every turn in life, yours and others, and how to and how not to deal with situations, gives you that maturity.
Sometimes even fiction provides that learning.

The notion that age is directly proportionate to maturity is often a cultural construct. In many societies, age is equated with wisdom and experience, while youth is sometimes dismissed as naive or impulsive. However, maturity stems not from the number of years lived but from the lessons learnt and the willingness to grow from every experience. Modern-day challenges, along with the unprecedented access young people have to information, perspectives, and lived experiences from across the world, mean younger generations often display emotional intelligence and adaptability far beyond their years. At the same time, older individuals may cling to outdated mindsets, proving that maturity is more about perspective and growth than the number of years already lived. Acknowledging this helps bridge generation gap and fosters mutual respect, enriching societal cohesion.

Malala Yousafzai, the youngest Nobel Peace Prize laureate, exemplifies maturity beyond her years. At just seventeen, she displayed resilience and a profound understanding of global issues, advocating for girls' education at immense personal risk.

Mansukhbhai Prajapati, rural innovator from India, developed the MittiCool refrigerator in his later years, demonstrating how embracing failures and lessons over decades can bring profound insights.

Books such as *The Alchemist* (1988) by Paulo Coelho also inspire individuals by illustrating life's unpredictability and the importance of understanding oneself, regardless of one's age.

76

Parenting is more than just biology.

> It is important to be mature and grown-up enough to be a parent. An actual parent.
> Not just a biological one.
> So that you are responsible for another life.
> For another soul to be brought into this world.
> And to care for and provide as much as you can.

Parenthood is often romanticized as a natural milestone, but being biologically capable of having children does not necessarily prepare one for the emotional, mental and moral responsibilities of raising a child. Across cultures, becoming a parent is seen as a rite of passage, yet the societal pressures to have children can sometimes overshadow the introspection needed to ensure readiness. True parenthood requires maturity, patience, and the ability to prioritize someone else's wellbeing over one's own. It is about creating an environment of safety, love and opportunity for a child to thrive in, regardless of personal limitations or societal expectations. Recognizing this helps build a generation that is nurtured not just physically, but emotionally and morally.

Indian entrepreneur Arunachalam Muruganantham,

known for revolutionizing menstrual hygiene in rural India, illustrates this ethos beautifully. Though he and his wife had no children at the time, he took on a father-like role for millions of girls and women, driven by the desire and sense of responsibility to improve their lives. When tragedy struck in 1997 with the Uphaar Cinema fire in New Delhi, Neelam Krishnamoorthy lost both her children. For many, such a loss would have been the end of all purpose, but for her, motherhood took on a new and unyielding form. Within weeks, she and her husband formed the Association of Victims of Uphaar Tragedy, becoming the voice for hundreds of bereaved families. For over two decades, she has fought relentlessly in courtrooms, not for personal closure alone, but to uphold a promise to her children that their lives—and their loss—would not be in vain. In doing so, she became a parent to an entire community's grief, showing that true parenthood is measured not by biology but by the courage to protect, nurture, and fight for others even when your own heart has been shattered.

Lesser-known examples include rural communities where elderly women, often referred to as 'village grandmothers', assume the role of moral and social parents, nurturing children with wisdom passed down through generations.

77

If you don't love yourself the most, who will?

In a world that constantly measures us by applause and approval, the truest validation is the kind we give ourselves. Perhaps the gentlest, yet most challenging, part of self-love is recognizing the quiet betrayals we sometimes make against ourselves—the moments we set aside our own needs to keep others comfortable, the times we tuck away our dreams because we are afraid they might be laughed at, or when we repeat our flaws so often that they start to feel like our whole story. These small, almost invisible acts of self-abandonment slowly chip away at our confidence. True self-love begins when we notice these patterns with kindness, not criticism, when we forgive the version of ourselves who did the best they could at the time, and when we find the courage to write a kinder, truer story. In many ways, it is simply a series of quiet reconciliations with our own heart.

For many years, I didn't like myself very much at all and craved outside validation. I was angry at the world for the bad hand I'd been dealt. I had no idea that *I had chosen the cards*!

Self-love is often misunderstood, especially in cultures where humility and selflessness are emphasized as virtues. However, loving oneself isn't about arrogance or selfishness; it's about recognizing your own worth and treating yourself with the respect and care you would offer to others. In a world saturated with social media and material aspirations, many people chase external validation, forgetting that true confidence must come from within. This self-acceptance becomes the foundation for healthier relationships, improved mental health, and building resilience for facing life's challenges. In societies that encourage self-love, individuals are more likely who are not only more content but also capable of contributing positively to their communities.

American entrepreneur Sophia Amoruso, founder of Nasty Gal, turned her early struggles into a journey of self-discovery, building her brand while learning to value herself beyond societal judgements.

Indian rural artisan communities often showcase this self-love through their work. A young Madhubani artist once revealed that her intricate art wasn't just about earning a livelihood, it was about honouring her identity and heritage, even when her work was initially dismissed by outsiders.

Another example is the life of Victor Frankl, a Holocaust survivor and psychiatrist, and the founder of logotherapy, who emphasized finding meaning and value in oneself despite unimaginable external hardships.

78

Be debt-free.

Pay off your credit card bills every month and be debt-free.
If you can live well, without even a credit card, do so.
Plan your personal finances and budgets.
Have adequate insurance coverage for yourself, your family, unemployment, property and possessions.
Life's biggest sense of independence comes from being debt-free, and having money to pursue your dreams.

In today's world, where consumerism often dictates lifestyle choices, the concept of being debt-free holds immense significance. Societies driven by material aspirations encourage borrowing to achieve instant gratification, leading many into financial distress. Being debt-free is not merely a financial goal; it represents freedom, independence, and the ability to make life's decisions without external pressures.

Culturally, this principle is deeply rooted in traditional practices where living within one's means was considered virtuous. However, while modern financial systems often normalize debt as a tool for progress, following the discipline to remain debt-free is an act of self-respect that ensures long-term security. It also allows individuals to focus on personal goals and emergencies without added stress, fostering peace of mind.

The legendary Indian industrialist J.R.D. Tata was known for his fiscal prudence, meticulously planning his ventures without over-leveraging, ensuring financial stability for his business empire and his workers.

Author and environmentalist Wendell Berry has spoken about living simply and sustainably on his farm in Kentucky, choosing a debt-free life over modern-day financial dependencies.

79

Start your retirement plan as soon as you finish college and start working.

I wish I knew this trick. I made the mistake of being ignorant about personal finances until I was thirty-eight.

Your decisions regarding your life and career will be very different when you are financially independent.

Retirement planning, though often dismissed by the young, is a cornerstone of long-term financial wellbeing. In cultures that place a strong emphasis on familial or governmental support for the elderly, the changing socioeconomic landscape has made self-reliance a necessity.

Starting early allows individuals to benefit from compounding, thereby creating a significant corpus with small investments. Moreover, financial independence reshapes life decisions—whether it's the freedom to switch careers, take a sabbatical, or pursue passion projects without monetary stress. Early planning also alleviates the burden on future generations, ensuring that the elderly can age with dignity and security. In a world increasingly leaning towards individualistic lifestyles, this lesson is both pragmatic and all-important.

A notable example is Radhika Gupta, CEO of Edelweiss Asset Management, who has openly spoken about the importance of financial literacy and planning. She credits her early education on managing finances—starting at the age of twenty-two—with laying the foundation for her current success. Gupta's story is a powerful reminder that understanding and investing early for retirement or for future needs can have a lasting impact on one's career trajectory.

80

Make peace with your past, so it won't spoil the present.

Let it rest.
Let it heal.
Let it stop knocking at your door.
You are not that person anymore.
You are not in that place anymore.
You owe the past no more rent.

Making peace with your past is a fundamental life lesson rooted in emotional maturity and self-awareness. In the social and cultural context of India, where familial ties and traditions are very important, letting go of past mistakes and grievances can be especially challenging. The idea of reputation, too, plays a significant role in shaping one's actions, often overshadowing personal growth. However, in an increasingly individualistic world, it is crucial to recognize that peace of mind and forward momentum come when we stop dwelling on the past. Safeguarding your reputation is important, but the tendency to protect it at all costs should not allow your ego or past failures to consume the present. Life is about finding balance—acknowledging past mistakes without letting them define us, and simultaneously understanding that your actions and thoughts today matter more than any past embarrassment.

A noteworthy example of making peace with one's past is the life of Dhirubhai Ambani, founder of Reliance Industries. Ambani had humble beginnings and faced many setbacks early in his career, including an initial lack of formal education and financial struggles. However, he never allowed those early challenges to dictate his future. Instead of dwelling on past mistakes, Ambani focused on building his business empire. His reputation, which he built with immense hard work and innovation, allowed him to become one of India's most influential entrepreneurs, showing that how you deal with the past determines how you move forward.

Amitabh Bachchan is known for his ability to bounce back from personal and professional setbacks. In the early 2000s, Bachchan faced a series of career failures, including the collapse of his business ventures. Instead of letting these failures consume him, he rebranded himself as a television host, and through perseverance, reinvented his career. His story is a shining example of making peace with past failures, ensuring they do not dictate the narrative of one's life moving forward.

81

Ride out the storm.

Greet every so-called disaster in your life with these words: 'This time next year, will this matter?'

Crises are stressful.

They are like tsunamis.

You cannot fight them.

But you can hold on firm. And ride out the storm.

In a society where success is often measured by how quickly one can overcome adversity, this life lesson urges individuals to acknowledge that setbacks are a part of life's natural rhythm. Instead of trying to fight every crisis, it's important to understand that some situations are beyond control, but how we respond to them is what ultimately defines us. In the Indian context, where expectations from family and society can sometimes create enormous pressure, the ability to approach crises with calmness and perspective is an invaluable skill. By asking oneself, 'Will this matter next year?', individuals can distance themselves from emotional stress, gaining the clarity to approach the situation with a level head. This mindset not only helps mitigate immediate stress but also in cultivating long-term resilience and emotional wellbeing.

Howard Schultz, former CEO of Starbucks, faced

numerous challenges while building the company. One of the most significant crises he faced was when the company was on the verge of bankruptcy in the early 2000s. Instead of succumbing to the pressures of failure, Schultz focused on the long-term vision, reframing the crisis as a temporary setback. He famously said, 'This is the moment we decide to turn the company around,' rather than letting the situation define Starbucks' future. Schultz's ability to ride out the crisis turned the company into a global powerhouse.

In India, Kiran Mazumdar-Shaw, founder of Biocon, faced many financial and institutional hurdles while establishing her company. In an industry where the odds were stacked against her, from scepticism about a woman leading a biotechnology firm to difficulties in securing funding and lab space, Mazumdar-Shaw often found herself in a crisis. However, instead of dwelling on the challenges, she embraced the philosophy of persistence and patience.

82

Save all natural resources.

Save electricity. Save water.
Shut your unused lights, fans, ACs, computer, TV, etc., at home and in office.
Save water. Shut that tap when not in use.

As we age, and as we become financially stronger, we ignore the basics of what we grew up with—saving all resources and not being frivolous about anything.

Once, there was a deep-rooted practice of thrift—turning off lights when not in use, reusing water, and being mindful of how much energy was consumed. However, with the rise of consumerism and technological advances, this mindset is slowly fading. As we advance in life, we tend to focus more on what we can afford rather than being mindful of the basics we once adhered to. The need to conserve energy, water, and other resources is no longer just an environmental responsibility, but a moral one, ensuring that future generations have access to the resources that we often take for granted.

This life lesson calls for a return to simplicity, reminding us that sustainability is rooted in small, daily actions that make a long-term difference.

Baba Amte, the famous social activist, dedicated his life to the rehabilitation of leprosy patients. Living in the remote forests of Maharashtra, he built Anandwan, a self-sustained village for leprosy patients and other marginalized groups. Baba Amte focused not only on rehabilitation but also on being resourceful.

The community at Anandwan reuses water, recycles materials, and grows its own food, setting a powerful example of sustainable living, even in a rural context.

Madhav Gadgil, an ecologist and environmentalist, has advocated the conservation of India's natural resources, particularly its water and forests. As Head of the Western Ghats Ecology Expert Panel, Gadgil has consistently highlighted the importance of preserving biodiversity and reducing the consumption of natural resources. His research and initiatives, including promoting sustainable farming practices, are grounded in his belief that long-term sustainability depends on the responsible use of resources by communities. He has been instrumental in raising awareness about the ecological importance of conserving India's natural wealth.

83

Travel tips are needed.

Use the loo when you have access to it, even if you don't feel the urge.

Charge your phone when you have access to a charger and charging point, even if your phone is charged ninety per cent.

Fill your drinking water bottle, when you have access to a refilling source.

These are not just habits for travellers, they are habits for life. The road—whether it winds through the chaos of Old Delhi, the emptiness of the mountains, or the polished and crowded airport—teaches you that comfort and preparedness rarely arrive exactly when you need them. Travelling through India and across the world, I have learnt that those who anticipate needs before they become urgent are the ones who travel lighter in spirit. It is about respect for your needs and comfort. You do not wait to be dehydrated to seek water, you do not wait for the battery to flash red to find a socket, and you do not wait until desperation strikes to find a restroom.

This mindset has saved me countless times. Once, on a domestic flight, the washrooms ran out of water within hours. On another business trip, a dying phone battery could have cut me off from the guide who was waiting at a crowded town marketplace. A quick top-up at a roadside dhaba earlier that day, though I did not need it then, meant I could still call for directions when the fog closed in.

I have also learnt smaller tricks that make travel smoother. Keep a fruit or a light snack handy even if you think you will find food soon. Store an extra copy of your ID in a separate bag. Learn to carry a small cloth or scarf that works as a head cover in the sun, a shawl in the cold, or a pillow on an overnight bus. Use quiet moments, like waiting at a boarding gate, to check your maps or reconfirm bookings rather than scrolling mindlessly. These small acts of readiness mean you meet the unexpected with calm rather than chaos.

Travel will always test you. Your ability to look after tomorrow's self today is the most reliable travel insurance you will ever have.

In today's fast-paced world, while travelling has become quite commonplace, it also presents a variety of challenges. Often, in the rush, we forget to take small yet essential precautions that can save us unnecessary discomfort. The wisdom of planning ahead, taking care of basic needs even before the urgency arises, and ensuring our comfort in unfamiliar environments is invaluable.

In the Indian cultural context, it is important to be resourceful and prudent, especially in rural or remote settings, where basic facilities may be scarce. This life lesson underscores the importance of anticipating needs rather than waiting until it's too late, a skill that can make travel far smoother and less stressful.

84

Invest in a good perfume and deodorant all your life.

Pick a fragrance that suits your body type and stick to it.

It's a great investment.

Investing in a good perfume and deodorant is often overlooked, but in many cultures, fragrance plays a significant role in personal grooming and social identity. The right scent can enhance one's presence and leave a lasting impression, often speaking louder than words.

In a world where first impressions matter, a signature fragrance becomes a part of your personal brand. The cultural emphasis on cleanliness and pleasantness, especially in social and professional settings, underscores the importance of investing in quality products. Choosing a fragrance that complements your body type and personality is a subtle yet powerful form of self-care, one that signals respect for yourself and for those around you. It's an investment in your own self-esteem, and in a way, creates an invisible aura that people remember.

Among public figures, Shah Rukh Khan is often spoken of as the man who smells wonderful. Many of his co-stars have mentioned it in interviews. Khan himself has shared that he carefully layers two of his favourite perfumes to create a scent that is uniquely his. Over time, this has become part of his personal signature — an invisible yet unforgettable presence that lingers in memory long after he has left the room. It is a reminder that the right fragrance is not just about smelling good for others, but about carrying with you a quiet, confident aura in every workplace, social gathering, and personal interaction.

85

Purpose

It's hard to find.

Harder to hold on to.

That's why it is important.

Life without a purpose is senseless.

Find your purpose. Then your life will become full of colours and you will want more out of it.

Life is a rat race. Learn to play it. But without attachment.

Compete hard and fair. Even when you know that others might not be fair. Your purpose will help you.

In today's fast-paced world, a purpose in life can often feel like an elusive concept, especially amidst the chaos of daily life. The pressure to keep up with societal expectations—whether it's career advancement, material success, or social validation—can overshadow the quest for deeper meaning. Yet, a purpose is central to the human experience. It acts as a compass that guides one through life's challenges, providing clarity and direction even in the most uncertain times.

In cultures around the world, a purpose has often been seen as intrinsic to a fulfilled life, transcending mere achievement. Without it, life can feel incomplete and meaningless, no matter how much external success one accumulates. Finding a purpose involves introspection, aligning personal values with actions, and working towards something greater than oneself. When people find their purpose, their entire outlook changes, infusing everyday activities with meaning and motivating them to push boundaries without attachment to the outcome.

Mahatma Gandhi had a clear sense of purpose, grounded in the pursuit of truth and non-violence. This guided his decisions and actions throughout his life, including his leadership in India's independence movement. His commitment to his purpose allowed him to remain steadfast despite challenges.

Steve Jobs famously said that his purpose was to 'make a dent in the universe' through innovation. His unyielding focus on this purpose and vision led to the creation of Apple, changing the world of technology forever.

Another example comes from the world of sports: Mary Kom, the boxer from India, found purpose in her desire to represent her country at the global level despite facing gender bias and personal struggles. Her unwavering commitment to her purpose allowed her to rise to the top of her sport, becoming an inspiration to many.

86

Patience is a skill, tool and virtue.

Build it as early in life as possible.

We mistake impatience to be a sign of being young.

That is senseless thinking.

Build your patience as much as possible.

It will help you in any situation.

Don't show your emotions to others.

In a world increasingly dominated by instant gratification, the importance of patience is often overlooked. The rise of the digital media and the culture of immediacy have made many believe that quick results are the only path to success. However, true growth—in personal development, relationships, or professional endeavours—requires time. Patience is a skill that demands constant cultivating and is often seen as a virtue in those who understand that success cannot be rushed.

In many cultures, patience is not only about waiting; it's about enduring with grace, learning from setbacks, and giving things the time they deserve to flourish. It's often in moments of pause that clarity emerges, and the best decisions are made. Learning to master patience helps us remain composed in challenging situations, navigate stress, and avoid impulsive decisions, ultimately leading to better outcomes in life.

Known as the 'Father of the White Revolution in India', Dr Verghese Kurien's patience was key to transforming India's dairy industry. His long-term vision for the cooperative model of milk production and distribution faced numerous hurdles, including political opposition and logistical challenges. But his immense patience and belief in his mission led to the creation of Amul, one of India's most successful cooperatives.

87

Build a habit of asking questions.

Curiosity is one of your most powerful tools, especially in a world overflowing with information. Developing the habit of asking questions, not just accepting what you're told, opens doors to deeper understanding and clearer thinking.

Whether it's in the classroom or boardroom, with friends, or online, with your competitors or colleagues, don't hesitate to seek clarity and challenge assumptions. Asking questions will help you learn more effectively, spot errors before they become problems, and develop your own independent perspective. It's also a key skill for creativity and innovation, allowing you to explore new ideas and solutions. Remember, every expert started by asking 'Why?' or 'How?' The habit of inquiry will serve you well, making you a confident decision-maker and a lifelong learner.

Beyond facts, asking questions is essential to understanding yourself and the world around you. It encourages empathy by prompting you to consider others' viewpoints and motivations. In a time when social media can flood you with half-truths and opinions disguised as facts, questioning becomes your shield against misinformation and groupthink. It takes courage to question popular beliefs or challenge authority, but this courage builds intellectual independence and resilience.

Take Elon Musk, for instance, who constantly questioned conventional wisdom about electric cars, space travel, and renewable energy. His relentless curiosity and refusal to accept limitations have driven innovations that are changing the world. By developing this habit, you prepare yourself not only for personal success but also to be an active, thoughtful contributor to society's progress.

88

Never speak or message when you are angry or upset.

In today's world, where instant communication is at our fingertips, the impulse to respond immediately when upset or angry can be overwhelming. Whether through social media, text messages, or emails, sending an emotional response in the heat of the moment can lead to irreversible consequences. In Indian culture, there is a strong emphasis on maintaining one's composure and thinking before speaking. The importance of self-control in communication is not just a moral virtue but a practical skill for fostering long-term relationships, both personal and professional. Learning to pause, reflect, and then respond thoughtfully is crucial to maintaining dignity and avoiding misunderstandings, making this life lesson both a cultural and emotional necessity in the modern age.

Mahatma Gandhi's principle of ahimsa or non-violence extended beyond physical actions to include words. Known for his calm approach, Gandhi often practised silence during times of deep frustration or anger. For instance, during protests or when addressing difficult issues, he would sometimes withdraw into silence rather than make rash statements that could escalate tension. His restraint in speech was an essential tool in his leadership, demonstrating the power of thoughtful communication.

89

Resilience

It's a fine personal virtue to have.
Bounce back from failures, hardships, depression, poor health, lack of resources, etc.
Nothing is permanent. Neither hardships, nor success.

We rarely ask ourselves, 'Why did I succeed?' Instead, we simply believe it's because of our hard work and abilities. But when things go wrong, we often ask, 'Why am I struggling even though I've done so much?'

Resilience is a word so fundamental, and yet so profound, that it deserves an entire page dedicated to its meaning and practice. In a world where change is the only constant, and uncertainty often seems overwhelming, resilience is not merely a trait but a vital skill for enduring life's inevitable ups and downs. It is the invisible force that enables us to recover from failure, hardship, illness and loss, and to continue moving forward with strength and grace.

Learn to accept and move on. Resilience is what successful people must have to make their success last. At the same time, while we only see their success, they still have their own challenges and problems.

Resilience is a timeless virtue that has been

emphasized in cultures worldwide, including India, where ancient scriptures and folklore often glorify the ability to rise above adversity. In a rapidly changing world fraught with uncertainties, resilience has become a critical skill to navigate personal and professional challenges. Whether dealing with financial hardships, health crises, or emotional setbacks, the ability to adapt and bounce back is what defines long-term success and personal growth.

In Indian culture, resilience is closely tied to the philosophy of impermanence, as encapsulated in phrases like 'Yeh waqt bhi guzar jayega (This too shall pass).' By cultivating resilience, individuals learn not only to endure hardships but also to grow stronger and wiser through them, creating a foundation for a balanced and fulfilling life.

Often referred to as India's 'original slumdog millionaire', Kalpana Saroj grew up in a Dalit family and faced systemic discrimination, personal tragedy, and abject poverty. Resilience became her greatest asset as she took on multiple jobs to survive and eventually rebuilt her life to become chairperson of Kamani Tubes. Saroj's story exemplifies the transformative power of persistence and determination.

Viktor Frankl, a Holocaust survivor and author of *Man's Search for Meaning* (1946), endured unimaginable suffering in concentration camps during World War II. His philosophy of finding meaning in life, even amidst great adversity, is a profound lesson in resilience. He used his experiences to inspire millions to go through their struggles with dignity and purpose.

90

Take the wins.

They are blessings.
They are glimmers of hope.
You won't have wins all the time.
But take each of those wins as positive reiteration of you.

Taking the wins, no matter how small, is a practice rooted in gratitude and optimism. In a world where challenges often overshadow successes, recognizing and celebrating wins allows us to stay motivated and grounded. Victories—personal or professional—are often celebrated as blessings from a higher power, reinforcing the idea that success is transient and should be cherished. The notion of savouring wins is closely tied to positive psychology, where acknowledging accomplishments can boost self-esteem and resilience. Wins, however fleeting, act as reminders of our capabilities and serve as stepping stones for greater achievements. They provide hope in times of struggle and inspire us to keep striving for more.

In his journey to revolutionize multiple industries, Elon Musk faced significant failures, from the early struggles of Tesla to SpaceX rockets exploding during tests. Yet, he celebrated every incremental success, such as the first successful rocket landing, as a massive victory, inspiring his teams to continue innovating. His ability to focus on wins, even when surrounded by setbacks, highlights the importance of positivity and persistence.

Indian environmentalist Saalumarada Thimmakka, who began planting trees as an act of love and purpose, found her wins in every sapling that thrived. With over 8,000 trees planted today, she reminds us that victories can be as small as nurturing life and watching it grow. Her wins weren't grandiose but deeply fulfilling, showcasing that even small achievements can define a legacy.

Born without limbs, motivational speaker and author Nick Vujicic has made a career out of highlighting how every small win—learning to write, swim, or live independently—can become a source of immense joy and gratitude. His life demonstrates that wins are not about scale but about the effort and spirit behind them.

91

Being mentored

Consider yourself lucky if someone mentors you.
As long as they are guiding you to the right values.
How will you know if it is the right value?
Trust your inner voice.

Mentorship is the cornerstone of personal and professional growth, deeply rooted in human tradition. In cultures worldwide, mentorship has been revered, whether as the guidance of gurus in ancient India or as master-apprentice relationships in trade and the arts. A mentor's influence goes beyond imparting skills; it involves shaping character, instilling values, and providing a compass for navigating life's complexities. However, the true impact of mentorship lies in aligning the mentor's teachings with one's inner voice, ensuring the values imparted resonate deeply. In an age of constant change, a good mentor is invaluable—a lighthouse guiding us through the storms of uncertainty, helping us grow with purpose and direction.

Steve Jobs credited Robert Friedland, an orchard owner and spiritual seeker, with inspiring his early ideas about aesthetics and spirituality. Jobs was influenced by Friedland's Zen-like philosophies, which shaped Apple's minimalist design ethos. This mentorship demonstrates how unconventional sources can impart profound lessons that influence a lifetime.

Leslie Auchincloss, founder of Biocon Biochemicals in Ireland, mentored Kiran Mazumdar-Shaw, the founder of Biocon Limited, India's leading biopharmaceutical company, in her early years. He encouraged her to take risks and provided her with the first platform to manufacture enzymes in India. This guidance laid the foundation for her journey to becoming one of India's most successful entrepreneurs.

92

Privacy

> Fight hard for yours.
> It will come with your values and behaviour while others try to invade it.
> In the digital world, nothing you say or write is private. Someday, someone could use it against you.

Privacy is one of the most undervalued yet essential aspects of modern life, especially in the digital age. Societies have placed importance on personal boundaries, understanding that privacy fosters individuality, security, and the freedom to think, express and act without undue scrutiny. Today, with the proliferation of social media, surveillance and data collection, protecting one's privacy is an ongoing battle. It's not just about physical or personal space anymore; it's about safeguarding your digital footprint. Missteps in online communication, often perceived as private, can lead to damage to one's reputation or worse. Privacy, therefore, is not merely a right but a responsibility, requiring conscious effort to maintain, particularly as it is intertwined with one's values and actions. Fighting for personal boundaries is essential to protect your mental and emotional wellbeing, ensuring that others respect your individuality and choices. Without clear boundaries, your time, energy and privacy can be exploited, leading to stress and a loss of self-identity.

Aria was a software engineer, known for her integrity and straightforward nature. Her life took an unsettling turn when her colleagues began sharing details about her personal life—gleaned from her social media accounts—during office gossip. She realized her openness online had unwittingly invited unwelcome scrutiny. Determined to reclaim her privacy, Aria deleted her personal accounts, restricted access to her phone number, and politely but firmly drew boundaries at work, refusing to entertain personal questions. Initially, she faced ridicule for being 'secretive', but over time, her colleagues respected her stance. By safeguarding her personal life, Aria found peace, avoided unnecessary drama, and stayed true to her values in both her professional and personal spheres. This Aria could be you or me!

93

Being friendly and being a friend are different.

It could happen at work. Your boss might be friendly, but most likely is not your friend.

In today's interconnected world, understanding the distinction between being friendly and being a friend is crucial for navigating both personal and professional relationships.

Friendliness is a social skill, a way to build rapport, a network, or maintain a positive atmosphere, especially in professional settings. However, friendship goes deeper, requiring trust, shared values, and mutual investment over time. In hierarchical or work environments, friendliness is often mistaken for friendship, leading to misplaced expectations and potential disappointments. A clear understanding of this difference can help manage relationships with appropriate boundaries, fostering healthy interpersonal dynamics without overstepping or misinterpreting intentions.

Indian entrepreneur Harsh, who runs a mid-sized startup, learnt this lesson early in his career. His former boss, who was always cordial and supportive during office hours, rarely showed interest in deeper matters outside of work. Harsh once approached him with a personal financial crisis, assuming their camaraderie would translate into tangible help. While his boss gave sound professional advice, he drew the line at personal involvement, leaving Harsh disillusioned but wiser.

A diplomat shared how she cultivated friendly yet professional relations at summits but kept her circle of personal friends separate to avoid conflict of interest. This clarity helped her navigate delicate situations, while remaining approachable yet professionally uninvolved.

These examples highlight how recognizing the line between friendliness and friendship ensures trust and balance in varied interactions.

94

Never doubt yourself.

The world will want to confuse you and make you feel lesser than what you are—as a person with potential and as a performer.

It's okay to wonder what makes the world want do so, but just don't doubt yourself.

I have seen long periods of failures and slowdown, when things just did not go through. Despite everything, the only thing that kept me going was not doubting myself.

Self-doubt is one of the greatest hurdles individuals face in an increasingly competitive and opinion-driven world. From social media to workplace pressures, constant comparisons and external judgements often undermine confidence, leaving even the most capable people questioning their abilities. However, self-belief is the foundation of growth and resilience. It allows individuals to filter out unnecessary noise and focus on their true potential.

This life lesson resonates universally, as it empowers people to stand firm in their decisions, trust their journey, and define success on their own terms. In a society that frequently tries to shape individuals with external validation, holding on to self-belief is a quiet act of rebellion and strength.

When Ritesh Agarwal started OYO, many doubted the feasibility of his business model, especially given his young age and lack of a college degree. People questioned his ability to manage a global hospitality company, but Ritesh's belief in his vision kept him going. Today, OYO has become a global brand, proving that self-belief can help overcome scepticism and pave the way for success.

Oprah Winfrey was told early in her career that she didn't have the 'look' or 'style' to succeed in television. She was even fired from her first reporting job. However, she never doubted her talent or her unique ability to connect with people. Her self-belief helped her build an unparalleled media empire and become a global icon of empowerment.

95

Be there for your core people.

No matter what.
Irrespective of time or distance, just be there for them.
Be it your family, friends, colleagues.
Whoever is in your core circle.
Nothing else matters.
Just be there.

In an increasingly individualistic world where priorities often shift towards personal ambitions and digital connections, the importance of standing by one's core people—family, close friends and trusted companions—has only grown. Societies across the globe emphasize the value of relationships, but the hustle of modern life often causes people to drift apart. Being there for your core people demonstrates loyalty, compassion and shared humanity, forming a support system that helps individuals navigate challenges and celebrate triumphs. These connections are not just emotional safety nets but the very essence of meaningful living.

When E. Sreedharan, the 'Metro Man of India', faced criticism and pressure during the Delhi Metro project, his core team of engineers and associates stood by him steadfast. Sreedharan was equally devoted to his team, providing guidance and support during difficult phases. This mutual solidarity ensured the project's success and set new benchmarks for urban transportation in India.

When Nelson Mandela was imprisoned on Robben Island for twenty-seven years, his wife, Winnie Mandela, stood by him despite the immense personal and political challenges she faced. Her unwavering presence and advocacy for his release kept his spirit alive and strengthened the global anti-apartheid movement. While their personal relationship faced complexities, Winnie's role as a pillar of support demonstrated the power of being there for one's core people, no matter the odds.

96

Sleep.

Catch up on quality sleep.
It's important for your health.
It's a life saver.

In today's hyperconnected world, sleep has become a casualty of ambition and lifestyle. People sacrifice rest for work, socializing, or screen time, considering it a sign of productivity to be sleep-deprived. However, the importance of quality sleep can never be overstated—it is the foundation of physical health, emotional wellbeing and mental clarity. Across cultures, the value of sleep is recognized in proverbs and practices, but modern-day pressures often lead people to neglect it. Reclaiming a healthy sleep schedule is essential for longevity and overall health.

The power of sleep lies in its ability to enhance cognitive function, improve memory, boost immunity and maintain emotional wellbeing. It is during sleep that the brain processes and organizes the vast amounts of information we absorb every day, enabling creativity, problem-solving and better decision-making.

However, the need for sleep is not a one-size-fits-all concept—it depends on the individual. While one person may thrive on six hours of sleep, another may require eight hours to function optimally. Finding the right balance is critical, as too little sleep leads to exhaustion, irritability, and even chronic health conditions, while excessive sleep can dull the mind and the body.

Listening to one's body and respecting its unique requirements for rest is a vital step toward achieving harmony in life. Sleep, when prioritized, becomes a powerful ally in navigating the complexities of modern-day existence.

The global entrepreneur Arianna Huffington had a wake-up call after collapsing from sleep deprivation early in her career. She later founded Thrive Global, advocating for prioritizing sleep and wellness.

Dr Devi Shetty, the renowned cardiac surgeon and founder of Narayana Health, emphasizes the importance of sleep for peak performance and long-term health. Despite his demanding schedule, he has consistently advocated for doctors and medical professionals to prioritize adequate sleep to avoid errors during surgeries and critical care. Dr Shetty himself ensures he gets sufficient rest, recognizing that a tired mind could lead to mistakes in a life-or-death situation. His belief in the restorative power of sleep extends to his leadership, where he encourages his team to balance their workload with sleep to ensure they remain sharp and attentive in their high-pressure roles.

97

Trust your gut feeling.

It's the universe's way of signalling what you subconsciously know and feel.

Often, events unfold around us that seem completely unrelated to what we're experiencing, and yet, somehow they hold a deeper meaning or connection.

Gut feeling, often dismissed as mere intuition, is rooted in a blend of subconscious analysis, past experiences and instinctual awareness. In a world focused on data, logic and facts, trusting your intuition might feel old-fashioned, but it quietly leads you through moments of uncertainty and when the full picture isn't clear. Cultures worldwide, especially in India, have long revered this 'sixth sense', attributing it to an inner connection with the universe or with one's higher self. Gut feelings act as the bridge between logic and emotion, offering insights that the conscious mind may not fully grasp. In an unpredictable world, relying on these instincts can provide clarity, confidence, and a deeper sense of alignment with one's purpose.

Steve Jobs was famous for trusting his intuition when making critical decisions. From the design of the iPhone to the development of Pixar, Jobs believed in the power of gut feeling to guide him. He often said that intuition is more powerful than intellect because it taps into life's interconnectedness, allowing people to see patterns that pure logic cannot, and take those significant leaps.

98

It's darkest before dawn.

Indeed, life follows a similar rhythm.
When the chips are down, and everything looks bleaks, trust yourself.
Talk to yourself, as many around you would have disappeared.
Give yourself positive messages.
I tell myself that no hardship lasts forever.

The biblical saying 'It's darkest before dawn' reflects the universal experience of going through tough times, where it feels as though things will never improve. In many philosophical systems, including Indian philosophy, hardship is often seen as a phase that is temporary, meant to build mental resolve and character. Enduring tough times in the belief that things will improve is deeply embedded in the collective consciousness.

The cultural significance of enduring challenges with patience and perseverance is also closely linked to values like self-reliance and hope, which are ingrained in the social fabric. The lesson of holding on during the darkest moments resonates strongly in a world driven by instant gratification, but true growth and transformation often come through overcoming adversity.

Mahendra Singh Dhoni, former captain of the

Indian cricket team, exemplified this lesson in the ICC World T20 in 2007. India had struggled through the tournament, and during the final match, it seemed like victory was slipping away. Yet, Dhoni remained calm, keeping faith in his strategy and team. His leadership through that intense pressure exemplified the belief that even in the darkest moments, endurance and trust can turn things around. Staying composed and believing that challenges would pass was a powerful motivator for both him and his team.

After being ousted from Apple, the company Steve Jobs founded, he went through a period of intense personal and professional turmoil. During this dark phase, he founded NeXT and acquired Pixar, both ventures that eventually led to his return to Apple and to the revolutionary products that followed. Despite the uncertainty, Jobs continued to remind himself that setbacks were just temporary.

99

Never allow anyone to control your emotions.

If you can master how you feel, and how you react or act on those emotions, without anyone controlling them, then you have gained mastery over the most difficult part of life.

With this attribute, you can win battles and overcome the biggest obstacles in life.

Not allowing others to control your emotions is an important theme in many cultures, especially in the context of personal empowerment. In a world where external influences—from family, society, or even the workplace—often shape our reactions and emotional responses, learning to maintain control over our emotions is an essential skill.

In Indian culture, this aligns with the teachings of self-control and *sattva* (mental purity) found in ancient texts like the Bhagavad Gita, where mastering one's emotions is seen as a path to inner peace and wisdom. This concept ties into psychological theories of emotional intelligence and resilience, where individuals who can regulate their emotions are more successful in navigating challenges, building relationships, and achieving long-term personal growth.

Nelson Mandela is the quintessential example of someone who never allowed others to control his emotions. Despite being imprisoned for twenty-seven years under the apartheid regime, Mandela maintained remarkable emotional control. He did not let hatred or bitterness consume him, even when he was subjected to the most brutal treatment. His ability to forgive and stay focused on his larger vision of ending racial segregation and discrimination against the Black majority in South Africa was a testament to the power of emotional mastery. Mandela famously said, 'Resentment is like drinking poison and then hoping it will kill your enemies.' His emotional strength was key in leading South Africa through a peaceful transition to democracy.

100

Miracles do happen.

Sometimes, life surprises us in ways that feel nothing short of miraculous.

While angels might be seen as symbols of hope and protection, the true miracles often come from within, through persistence, faith, and the quiet strength to keep going when all seems lost. My life has shown me enough to believe that miracles are real, that they show up as unexpected breakthroughs born from steadfastness and belief.

Miracles, then, are as much about the unseen power within us as they are about any external force. They invite us to trust in our own capacity to rise, believe, and create meaning even in the darkest moments.

In a world driven by logic, reasoning and the need for evidence, the belief in miracles often seems anachronistic. However, it is in those rare moments of serendipity, when everything aligns against the odds, that people experience what can only be described as a miracle.

Across cultures, including in Indian traditions, miracles are often understood not just as divine interventions, but as expressions of hope and grace that carry us through our darkest hours. They teach us that even when the path seems certain and planned, the unexpected can light the way forward.

Michael Phelps, the legendary American swimmer, embodies the possibility of miracles through his incredible career and personal struggles. Phelps overcame numerous obstacles, including depression, addiction and personal setbacks, only to rise to the top of his sport, winning twenty-three Olympic gold medals, the highest by any Olympian.

At his lowest point, after a publicized DUI arrest and battle with mental health issues, Phelps had every reason to give up. He credits his belief in himself and the support of his family and mentors for pulling him through. Phelps' recovery and triumph against all odds stand as a testament to the miraculous power of persistence, faith and belief in a higher purpose, despite personal darkness.

One of the most remarkable stories of belief in miracles is that of author J.K. Rowling. Besides being a single mother, Rowling's life was marked by other personal struggles, including financial hardship and depression. She recalls that the moment she reached her lowest point, with little hope for her future, was when she penned down the first book of Harry Potter. Her belief in the story and the strength to keep moving forward despite rejection after rejection is a testament to the power of perseverance and faith in miracles. The success of Harry Potter and the global impact of her work was nothing short of miraculous, turning her into one of the wealthiest and most influential women in the world.

101

Write your obituary.

Highlighting the way you have lived your life.
That's what your soul would be proud of.
It is proof that each living creature like us has a reason to be born on earth.

Even your own family will mourn your passing, and yet have a meal within a few hours of your departure. Life and living go on.

Writing your own obituary is a profound exercise that goes beyond contemplating the inevitable end of life. It is a conscious invitation to reflect on the essence of your existence, the values that guide your actions, and the impact you hope to leave behind. This life lesson encourages you to step outside the day-to-day rush, look at your life from a bird's-eye view, and ask yourself *not just how you wish to be remembered, but how you truly want to live.* It forces an honest evaluation of your legacy, prompting you to consider whether you are living in alignment with the principles you hold dear. The power of this exercise lies in its ability to highlight what truly matters: love, kindness, integrity, and the contribution you make to the world around you.

Writing your obituary is not about predicting the end, but about actively designing a life that reflects the best of who you are, ensuring that when the time comes, the story told about you will be one of purpose, authenticity and lasting impact. It serves as a reminder that our time here is finite, but the way we live it—through the choices we make, the people we affect, and the causes we champion—gives our life its deepest meaning.

When you are gone, memories of you live only through your deeds and the impact these would have had. That's what I strive for—*impact.*

To be recalled on the *final* day as:

'A learner. Kind, truthful. Gave it all. Did not expect anything in return. Great sense of humour. Had much to teach. Amazing human being.'

Epilogue

As we draw to a close this collection of life lessons—or life's secrets, it's tempting to think of them as words on a page, as wisdom from the past, easy to tuck away, maybe to revisit another day.

But here's the truth: these lessons are not static.

They are dynamic, alive, organic, evolving, waiting to be applied to each of us. And while they serve as a gentle guide, they aren't prescriptive.

They are designed to nudge you, to help you see beyond the ordinary, and to trigger your own questions, reflections and revelations.

Every individual has their own journey to make, their own story to tell. What worked for someone may not be your path; that's the magic of it all. This book is not a blueprint for a life that you must copy; it's a mirror—not only reflecting the experiences of others, but also offering an opportunity for you to ask yourself, 'What next? What is it that I need to do to live life on my own terms, with purpose and intention?'

Every life is a series of lessons, some learnt quickly, others taking longer to sink in. And each one shapes us, sometimes in ways we can't understand immediately. It's important to remember that you are in charge of the narrative of your life. No one else's story can be your own, and no one else's lessons are meant to define your journey. Embrace your individuality; your story is unlike any other. It's also important to acknowledge the stages of life that make these lessons resonate differently.

A young professional starting their career might find lessons about trusting their gut feeling particularly liberating, while someone approaching retirement might value the last lesson on leaving behind a meaningful legacy. This book is not just an attempt to offer guidance across age-groups and circumstances, it's also a gentle reminder that each of you will add your own wisdom to these pages—life's ultimate lessons will always be yours to discover.

You will face challenges, yes, but also experience moments of sheer brilliance and joy. The lessons you've read in this book are not about circumventing hard times, but about finding strength while going through them, seeing them as part of the ebb and flow of life.

Looking ahead, the future remains an unfolding mystery shaped by the choices we make today and the challenges that await us. While these lessons draw heavily on the wisdom of the past and present, it's vital to consider what the future will demand.

Adaptability will be essential. The rapid pace of change—in technology, work and society—requires us to be flexible without losing our core values. The willingness to learn, unlearn and relearn will keep us resilient in an unpredictable world.

Emerging technologies such as artificial intelligence, biotechnology, quantum computing, and automation promise to transform every aspect of our lives—from healthcare and education to how we connect and create. While these advances offer incredible possibilities, they also raise profound questions about ethics, privacy, and what it means to be human. Navigating this new terrain will require wisdom, thoughtful reflection, and a commitment to ensuring technology serves the greater good.

Sustainability will no longer be optional but a moral imperative. Protecting the environment and fostering social responsibility will shape how we live and coexist. Each individual's choices ripple outward, reminding us that collective wellbeing matters.

Authenticity in a hyperconnected world will be a critical challenge. Technology offers tremendous opportunity but also brings its share of risks—mental strain, misinformation and privacy loss. Finding balance through mindfulness and self-awareness will help us preserve our true selves.

Lifelong learning will be our greatest asset. With constant innovation reshaping knowledge and skills, curiosity and openness will allow us to stay engaged and relevant beyond traditional education.

Through all this change, human values remain the foundation. Integrity, kindness and compassion will guide us, no matter how complex or advanced the world becomes. The future will challenge us to uphold empathy and ethical decision-making, honouring the dignity of all.

So, as you move forward, remember, you are not bound by anyone else's definition of success or happiness. Seek the answers that are true for you, on your own terms. And know this—the best part of your journey is yet to unfold. With each new step, you have the opportunity to create the life that is uniquely yours, and in doing so, to inspire others to do the same.

There is no one-size-fits-all formula for living. There is only your path. Walk it boldly, with confidence in your own abilities, and with the understanding that your life is a story in the making. It's never too late to write the next chapter, and the future is yours to shape.

No one else can walk your path for you, and no one else's lessons will fully mirror your own. So, as you reflect on these pages, remember to look inward as well. Trust your experiences, your intuition, and the lessons life offers you. They are invaluable. So go ahead: be positive, be curious, and let the adventure called life unfold.

Acknowledgements

My gratitude:

To Kalyani, my North Star, thank you for the ego-free 'us' in our lives.

To the memory of my *thatha* and *pati*—the deep roots of my values. They shaped my core.

To my late mother for her grit and determination. Thank you, Amma, for making me believe, despite all odds.

For what life with my late father taught me. Thank you, Appa, for everything.

To the friends who have shown that life is more than just existential. Thank you for being you, when the chips were down.

To many others who journeyed into my life, with impact that moved me ahead and deep.

To yet others, who showed me the other side of life. Thank you. That helped me learn some life lessons quicker.

To Dibakar Ghosh and the team at Rupa Publications, for being kind, professional and efficient, and for believing in this book and bringing it to my readers.